A GOVERNOR
and
HIS IMAGE
in
BAROQUE BRAZIL

A Publication from the James Ford Bell Library
at the University of Minnesota

A GOVERNOR and HIS IMAGE in BAROQUE BRAZIL

The Funereal Eulogy
of Afonso Furtado de Castro
do Rio de Mendonça
by
Juan Lopes Sierra

Edited by STUART B. SCHWARTZ

Translated by RUTH E. JONES

UNIVERSITY OF MINNESOTA PRESS □ MINNEAPOLIS

Copyright © 1979 by the University of Minnesota.
All rights reserved.
Published by the University of Minnesota Press,
2037 University Avenue Southeast, Minneapolis, Minnesota 55455,
and published in Canada by Burns & MacEachern
Limited, Don Mills, Ontario

Printed in the United States of America
at the University of Minnesota Printing Department

The University of Minnesota is an equal opportunity
educator and employer.

Library of Congress Cataloging in Publication Data

Lopes Serra, João, 17th cent.
    A Governor and his image in baroque Brazil.
    Translation of Paneguirico funebre.
    Includes bibliographical references and index.
    1. Barbacena, Afonso Furtado de Castro do
Rio de Mendonça visconde de, d. 1675. 2. Brazil—
Governors—Biography. 3. Brazil—History—17th
century. I. Schwartz, Stuart B. II. Title.
F2528.B37L6613   981'.03'0924 [B]   78-27512
ISBN 0-8166-0879-2

PREFACE

In 1968 a Lisbon bookdealer placed on sale a manuscript entitled "Vida o Paneguirico funebre al Senor Affonso furtado castro do Rio de Mendomca" signed by Juan Lopes Sierra and dated 1676 in the "City of San Salvador Bahia de Todos Los Santos." That summer, the editor had the opportunity to examine the manuscript, and subsequently the James Ford Bell Library of the University of Minnesota purchased it. Upon further examination it was decided that because of the considerable historical interest of this work, its rarity (only one other copy is known to exist in the former royal library, the Biblioteca da Ajuda of Lisbon), and the vision it provides of life in late seventeenth-century Brazil, it should be made available to a wider public. In conjunction with the editor and translator, the James Ford Bell Library has incorporated this volume in its continuing series of publications on European expansion.

The manuscript itself is physically unimpressive. It measures 21 cm × 16 cm and is bound in modern vellum. It contains 112 unnumbered leaves. The paper is in excellent condition and the script is a neat and firm hand typical of the late seventeenth century. Occasional interlinear additions and an often confused orthography suggest that the manuscript is not the work of a professional scribe. It may well have been written, as the author states at the close of the prologue, in his own hand "at the age of seventy-two."

Because so little was known about Juan Lopes Sierra, the author of the "Paneguirico funebre," and about the hero of the work, Afonso Furtado de Castro do Rio de Mendonça, the editor began to collect pertinent materials on research trips to Portugal and Brazil from 1970 to 1974. Juan Lopes Sierra had been suggested as the author of a famous political tract of the late seventeenth century, the *Anti-catastrophe*, which dealt with the removal of King Afonso VI from the throne by his brother Pedro. The suggestion of his authorship was based on a letter signed by João Lopes Serra (the Portuguese form of Juan Lopes Sierra) in Bahia in 1671 which stated that he had written a work entitled "Antecatastrophe." The work itself had disappeared when the letter was brought to the attention of Camilo Aureliano da Silva e Souza, who published the famous political work in 1845. Souza, on the basis of internal evidence, rejected Lopes Serra as the author of the *Anti-catastrophe*, an opinion later shared by Gastão de Melo de Matos in a series of articles on the authorship of that work (Camilo Aureliano da Silva e Souza, editor, *A Anti-catastrophe, Historia d'Elrei D. Affonso 6° de Portugal* (Oporto, 1845), xx-xxii; Gastão de Melo de Matos, Sobre a "Anti-catastrophe," *Arquivo Histórico de Portugal*, 2 (1935), 127-37; 3 (1937-39), 96-120, 181-82). Neither Souza nor Melo de Matos was familiar with the "Paneguirico funebre." Had they been, they would have learned that Lopes Sierra was seventy-two years old in 1676. Because Melo de Matos demonstrated that the *Anti-catastrophe* was written between 1696 and 1700, Lopes Sierra's age argues against his authorship. Other than the suggestion of authorship in the Lopes Serra letter, there is no reference to him in discussions of Portuguese and Brazilian literature.

The editor did discover some information about the life and activities of Afonso Furtado. This material is incorporated in the introduction, appendixes, and notes.

In 1972 and again in 1974 the editor was able to consult the only other known version of the "Paneguirico funebre" in the Biblioteca da Ajuda in Lisbon. The two manuscript versions are very similar. The script of both appears to be the work of the same hand. The Ajuda copy has only 109 leaves and omits some sections contained in the Minnesota manuscript. Also, the organizational headings of the Ajuda version are different. Other discrepancies between the two manuscripts are minor. Word order is inverted in some places, and minor additions or deletions have been made in others. None of these variations alter the meaning or sense of the work. Therefore, since our purpose is to present the "Paneguirico funebre" as a historical document rather than as a work of literature, we have not discussed minor variations. The principal difference between the Minnesota and Ajuda manuscripts is the existence in the latter of three decorative acrostic poems, a very popular form in Iberian baroque literature. Also, this manuscript contains a sonnet not found in the Ajuda version. The Ajuda acrostic poems are reproduced in the notes section (see pages 192, 203-5).

A comparison of the two versions of the "Paneguirico funebre" leads us to believe that the Minnesota manuscript is the original, written in Bahia in 1676, and that the Ajuda document is a presentation copy enriched with additional poetry, a decorative frontispiece, and a more careful hand. This belief is supported by a textual reading of the two manuscripts. On page 4 of the Minnesota version is a reference to "the treaty of peace between *that* [*aquella*, italics added] and the Spanish crown." The use of *aquella* indicates that the writer is not in that place (i.e., Portugal). The Ajuda manuscript refers instead to "*this* [*esta*, italics added] and the Spanish crown." Therefore, it appears that the Minnesota manuscript originated in the City of Salvador and that the Ajuda version is a presentation copy prepared for the crown or for the author's patron, Antônio de Sousa e Meneses (the hero's nephew), and copied in Portugal. Finally, the three acrostic poems found in the Ajuda manuscript are written in Portuguese and the text is in Spanish, indicating that the poems are probably later additions.

The "Paneguirico funebre" presents more than the usual number of problems to the modern translator. The work is characterized by the complex syntax of Iberian baroque literature, with a strong penchant for digressive dependent clauses. Also, it contains a haphazard interchanging of orthographical symbols, which indicates that the author wrote words as he pronounced them. These problems and the author's tendency to run words together are common in manuscripts of the period. An added complication is that the author (presumably a longtime Spanish resident of Brazil), writing in Spanish about a Portuguese colony, occasionally corrupted normal Spanish forms and syntax with Portuguese linguistic elements. In addition, Brazilian and Portuguese place-names are often so garbled in the manuscript that only with considerable effort were they deciphered. Cachoeira, for example, is consistently written "Caxonera"; Covilhã becomes "Cuvillan." We have transposed place-names into the original language when possible. These problems seem to stem partly from the author's admitted lack of formal education and of familiarity with details of Portuguese and Brazilian geography.

Personal names present another problem. Lopes Sierra, writing in Spanish, altered Portuguese personal names so that, for example, João Matos de Aguiar became "Juan Mattos de Aguilar." We have converted all these to the form of the original language. We have, however, made an exception with the author's name, Juan Lopes Sierra. Assuming his Spanish nationality, the proper form should be "López" not "Lopes," but because of the strong possibility that the manuscript is a holograph, we have left his name as he probably wrote it himself. The hero's name presents a different problem. Modern Portuguese orthography calls for "Afonso" rather than "Affonso," as it was written in the seventeenth century. For the sake of uniformity we have adopted the modern usage throughout. We have, however, followed the governor's own signature in writing his full name as "Afonso Furtado de Castro do Rio de Mendonça," although contemporaries, including Lopes Sierra, sometimes omitted the final "de."

In typical baroque fashion, the author indexes and annotates the manuscript with marginal notes and observations, which are retained in the translation.

Our goal has been to produce a readable translation for a modern English-speaking audience, while maintaining the essence of the original. Brackets [ ] have been used freely to clarify the text for the reader. Punctuation has been altered or added for the sake of clarity. Still, the baroque syntax, especially in descriptions of the artistic elements associated with the funeral preparations, makes for complicated and difficult reading. Any attempt to eliminate all such difficulties for the modern reader, however, would be unfaithful to the form and feeling of the original. Hyperbole, digression, allegory, and verbosity are all characteristics of the baroque age of Iberian literature and to expunge them entirely would destroy the essence of the work.

During the preparation of this volume many friends and colleagues have provided suggestions and help. In Portugal, Mr. J. C. Silva shared his profound knowledge of Portuguese bibliography and nobility. In Brazil, Ms. Neuza Rodrigues Esteves supplied information on the Misericórdia of Bahia. Professor Pedro Calmon and the staff of the Historical Institute of Rio de Janeiro took time to answer inquiries, and Professor Fernando Novais of the University of São Paulo provided useful advice. Professor Dauril Alden of the University of Washington helped to clarify some obscure passages, and Mr. Lawrence "Bill" Towner of the Newberry Library provided an emergency reference service. Mr. Carl Hanson allowed us to use portions of his unpublished doctoral thesis on Portugal in the baroque era, and a similar favor was extended by Ms. Rae Flory. Mr. Morgan Broadhead provided considerable help in tracing Afonso Furtado's genealogy. A conversation with Professor C. R. Boxer revealed some bibliographic tips that we would surely have missed without his aid.

Professors Tom Kelly and John Evans and Mr. Marc Cooper, all historians of the ancient world in the Department of History at the University of Minnesota, guided us to the sources of some classical

PREFACE

references. Professors Anthony Zahareas and Nicholas Spaduccini of the Spanish Department provided useful leads to materials on Spanish literature. Ms. Rosa de la Cueva Peterson drew the map, and Ms. Tina Marin reviewed sections of the translation. The index was prepared by Mr. John Jenson, and Ms. Vicki Zobel typed the many drafts of the manuscript. A special note of thanks must go to the editor's wife, Nancy M. Schwartz, who with good humor and grace joined him in the archives of Portugal and Brazil during their first months of marriage. Her help and support have been indispensable. Research for this volume was carried out in part with the support of a grant from the Graduate School of the University of Minnesota. Finally, a special debt of thanks is due Ms. Carol Urness, Assistant Curator of the James Ford Bell Library. Her cooperation, exhortations, and efforts helped bring this project to completion.

Stuart B. Schwartz
Ruth E. Jones

July 1978

CONTENTS

Preface   v

Introduction   3

Life or Funereal Eulogy   ·31

Appendix A. Personalia   159

Appendix B. A Note on Portuguese and Brazilian Military Organization   173

Appendix C. Genealogy of Afonso Furtado   179

Appendix D. Currency, Weights, and Measures   182

Notes   187

Index   209

Illustrations

Details from door to the house of João de Matos de Aguiar   1, 157
Map of the Bahian Sertão in the XVIIth century   7
Pages from "Paneguirico funebre"   111, 131
His Highness Dom Pedro II   153
Escutcheon of viscounts of Barbacena   179
Genealogy of Afonso Furtado   180
Acrostic poems from "Paneguirico funebre"   203-5

Facing: Detail from door to the house of João de Matos de Aguiar, a prominent figure in colonial Bahia. The house no longer exists, but the door is on the building of the Ministry of Education in Salvador.

A GOVERNOR
and
HIS IMAGE
in
BAROQUE BRAZIL

INTRODUCTION

This volume presents a previously unpublished and virtually unconsulted manuscript history of the administration and death of a governor of Brazil in the late seventeenth century. Written by Juan Lopes Sierra, a mysterious figure about whom almost nothing is known, this panegyric biography has little intrinsic literary merit, falling into the genre of honorific and commissioned eulogy so typical of baroque literature in Spain and Portugal.

As a historical document, however, it has considerable interest. The manuscript deals with the actions, life, and death of Afonso Furtado de Castro do Rio de Mendonça, viscount of Barbacena and governor of Brazil (1671-75). Authored by an eyewitness to many of the events described, it provides heretofore unknown details about this governor's administration. Especially noteworthy are the observations on directing a series of military campaigns into the interior of Brazil for the purpose of subduing hostile Indian groups and searching for mineral wealth. In addition, the author's attention to details of religious life in the capital city of Salvador and his minute and seemingly endless description of the sumptuous preparations for and public ceremonies associated with the governor's burial reveal the spiritual, moral, and aesthetic concerns of the colonial elite and the tenor of life in baroque Brazil. Perhaps most important, the period covered is one of the least-studied epochs of the Brazilian past: a hiatus between the great century of sugar (1570-1670), when Brazil dominated the European market for that commodity, and the half-century of gold (1695-1750), when strikes in the south-central interior changed the economic and demographic configurations of the colony and for a short period gave the Portuguese metropolis a sense and the ephemeral reality of vast riches. Whatever the literary limitations of Juan Lopes Sierra, his work does weave together the themes of conquest and charity, the search for mines and the quest for salvation, and the fusion of politics and morality so revealing of the mental attitudes of the dominant groups in this colonial society.

HISTORICAL CONTEXT: BRAZIL IN THE SEVENTEENTH CENTURY

Early European interest in Brazil was limited primarily to the acquisition of brazilwood trees, which produced a valuable dye. After the European discovery of Brazil in 1500, Portuguese contacts were made by intermittent voyages of royal contractors and private individuals who cut wood on the coast or bartered with the Indians to do so. During these early years the route to India seemed far more important to Portugal than did the "Land of Parrots," as Brazil was sometimes called. But other countries were covetous: the intrusion of French interlopers eventually caused the Portuguese to alter their policy.

By the 1530s the Portuguese crown realized that control of the Brazilian coast could be secured only by permanent settlement. To that end the coastline was divided into large parcels and granted to Portuguese noblemen who in return for lordship agreed to settle and develop their "captaincies," as the grants were called. This experiment in state-sponsored private initiative produced mixed results. In most of the captaincies factional squabbling among the colonists and warfare with the Indians brought failure and disillusionment. But in a few areas where the cultivation of sugar cane had been successfully introduced, thriving plantation colonies began to grow. Lands were distributed to colonists, capital was found in Europe, and slaves, first Indian and then African, were brought to labor in the fields and mills. The sugar industry began to expand rapidly after 1560, especially in the northeastern captaincies of Pernambuco and Bahia. Bahia, in fact, had been chosen in 1549 as the site for the royal administrative capital and the city of Salvador had been constructed there as the seat of a governor general and other royal officials.

Throughout the seventeenth century sugar dominated Brazil's development. Most of the plantations were found within thirty miles of the coast, and the major cities were ports created to facilitate the commerce in sugar and slaves. The population was concentrated in the cities and near the sugar mills (*engenhos*), and to a large extent the colony of Brazil was a narrow strip of settled territory running from the mouth of the Amazon east, then south to the port of Santos. What expansion there was into the interior usually followed the few navigable rivers or the passes through the mountain ranges that hemmed much of the coast. The sugar industry's need for cattle—as food and transportation—stimulated some penetration into the interior, especially along the São Francisco River, where large cattle ranches were established. But, in the main, the rugged and forbidding topography of the interior (*sertão*), with its semiarid climate, and the European orientation of the major economic activity, sugar production, limited Portuguese interest in, and penetration of, the interior.

Then, too, there were the Indians. The major tribes of the coast, most of whom spoke the Tupí-Guaraní language, had been decimated by warfare, European disease, and enslavement before 1600.[1] Many peoples had fled into the interior, joining the nomadic hunters who inhabited the sertão. Although occasional expeditions of missionaries or slavers brought groups of Indians down to the Portuguese settlements, for the most part the tribes of the interior stiffly resisted the expansion of the colony and at times attacked the towns and plantations of the coast. This was especially true in the captaincies of the central coast—Bahia, Ilhéus, Porto Seguro, and Espirito Santo. Indians stubbornly resisted Portuguese efforts to reduce them to colonial control under either secular or religious administration, and such resistance was another effective barrier to the westward expansion of the colony.

A major exception to the coastal and export orientation of the colony was the town of São Paulo, located in the southern captaincy of São Vicente. São Paulo, one of the world's great cities today, was through most of its colonial history a small and insignificant town. Located about fifty miles from the coast on a high plateau, its inhabitants, the Paulistas, looked toward the interior. Poor in material wealth and heavily influenced by Indian customs, the Paulistas became the backwoodsmen of colonial Brazil. Their expeditions, called *entradas* or *bandeiras*, were organized to search for mineral wealth or to capture Indians who could then be used as domestic servants and agricultural laborers. Once beyond the city limits the Paulistas adopted the ways of the forest. Most spoke Tupí-Guaraní as well as or better than Portuguese and many were, in fact, *mestiços*, the children of Portuguese-Indian unions. In the early seventeenth century they raided the Jesuit missions in eastern Paraguay for Indian slaves and throughout the century groups of Paulistas and their Indian auxiliaries trekked across the interior of Brazil in search of mineral wealth and Indian captives. They established a deserved reputation as tough, often heartless, frontiersmen and Indian fighters who were independent-minded and troublesome, but good allies when the battle was hard. In time, their skills and experience were mobilized for the goals of the colonial government.

The administrative center of the colony, and the locale of most of the events described in the manuscript presented in this volume, was the captaincy of Bahia. It had been created as one of the grants in the system of royal donations sponsored by the crown. The cap-

A Governor and His Image in Baroque Brazil, Stuart B. Schwartz (editor) and Ruth E. Jones (translator). Copyright ©1979 by the University of Minnesota.

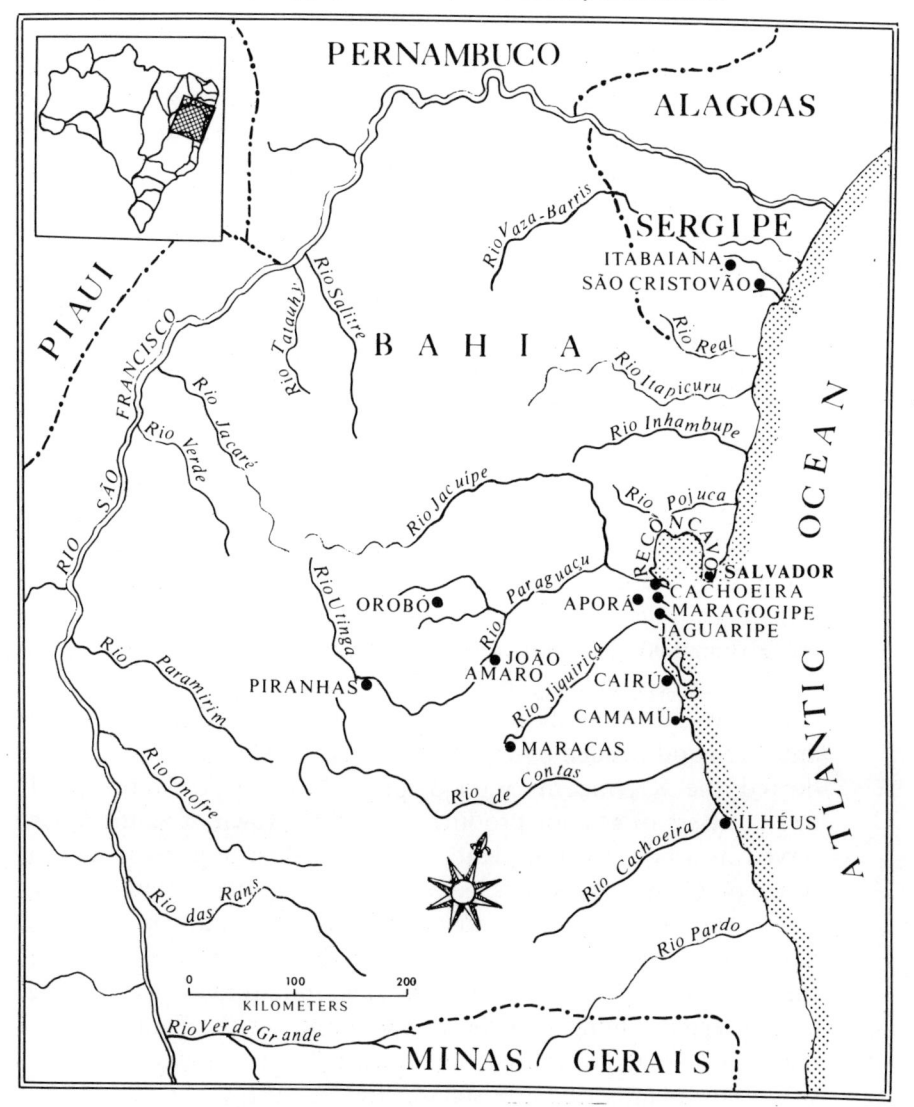

Bahian Sertão in the XVIIth Century

taincy was centered on the beautiful Bay of All Saints, long a haven for Portuguese and French dyewood traders on the coast. Although the donatary had succeeded in establishing a small settlement, his colony was torn by factional disputes, and upon his death at the hands of Indians in the area, the crown seized the opportunity to choose Bahia as the site of its colonial capital. A large expedition arrived in 1549 under the direction of Brazil's first governor general, and a city was built on a high escarpment overlooking the Bay of All Saints. The city, Salvador da Bahia de Todos os Santos, served as the seat of colonial power from 1549 until 1763, when the capital was moved to Rio de Janeiro. With a population in the seventeenth century of about 20,000, Salvador's importance was both administrative and commercial, the latter the result of the burgeoning sugar industry that developed in the rich lands, or *Recôncavo*, encircling the Bay of All Saints.

The Recôncavo was the economic core of Bahia. Along the rivers and on the margins of the northern and western reaches of the bay, many sugar plantations were established. By 1690 there were more than 100 engenhos in the Recôncavo and the population was over 35,000, including about 20,000 slaves. The southern areas were devoted primarily to food crops and to the supply of timber and firewood needed by the plantations. A number of small towns dotted the Recôncavo. Maragogipe and Jaguaripe, in the south, were centers of manioc production, and the town of Santo Amaro served as a port for the plantation zone. Most important was the town of Cachoeira, which had developed in a transition zone between the areas of sugar and manioc cultivation and was, by the late seventeenth century, the site of a flourishing tobacco agriculture. Moreover, Cachoeira had earned a reputation as "the entrance to the sertão," lying as it did at the mouth of the Paraguaçu, the major river that penetrated the interior. The town was, as we shall see in this manuscript, the staging area for many expeditions and forays.

South of the Bay of All Saints lay a humid zone with heavy rainfall and thick forests. This area, known as Ilhéus, was administratively subordinate to Bahia and, more important, was in many ways an economic appendage to it. Although some sugar was grown there, especially in the lower reaches of the rivers that ran to the coast, most of the land was unsuited for such agriculture. Instead, inhabitants of towns like Cairú, Camamú, and São Jorge dos Ilhéus devoted their activities to producing manioc, the basic staple of Brazil, and supplying timber and firewood to the sugar mills of the Recôncavo. In general, this region was sparsely settled and its inhabitants were much poorer than the planters of the Recôncavo. Life was also made difficult by the continual warfare carried out against groups of Indians like the Aimoré and Grens, who demonstrated remarkable resilience in the face of Portuguese power. The threat that continual Indian attacks posed to these settlements and to the supply of food and fuel for the sugar industry moved Portuguese administrators in Salvador to action. Much of Lopes Sierra's manuscript is a description of campaigns that resulted from the internecine warfare in the southern regions and the colonial government's desire to eliminate the problem.

The interior of Bahia during this period was defined by the São Francisco River, which flowed some 3,100 kilometers north and east in a great arc from its sources in Minas Gerais to empty into the sea about 380 kilometers north of Salvador. The region lying on the southern bank of the São Francisco, near the coast, was the separate captaincy of Sergipe de El-Rey, like Ilhéus, economically and administratively linked to Bahia. Some sugar was grown there along the rivers, especially near the town of São Cristóvão. More important, this region, like the area of Bahia lying just north of Salvador, became the center of an expanding stock-raising zone. Herds were pushed out along the São Francisco, the Rio Real and other rivers, and by the mid-seventeenth century there had been considerable penetration of the interior. But the approximately 500 kilometers that lay between Salvador and the São Francisco in a straight line due west was a land of mountain ranges, scrub brush, periodic droughts, and hostile Indians. Only occasional missionaries and slaving or mineral-hunting expeditions had traversed this territory, and with the exception of a few ranches and scattered settlements like Jacobina, the sertão of Bahia remained closed to occupation or effective colonial control. At the end of the seventeenth century, the French traveler Gabriel Dellon, who visited Bahia in 1676, described the situation as follows: "The Portuguese prompted by ambition to extend their borders send constantly abroad their parties who by degrees as they conquer these barbarians curb them by some forts they build in their new conquests. Whilst I was there I was credibly informed that they had extended their conquests above eighty leagues deep into the country."[2] The work presented here, despite its panegyric purpose and attention to other matters, is in large part a description of this movement: the opening of the interior as carried out by the governor of Brazil, Afonso Furtado, from 1671 to 1675 for the purpose of subduing the Indians and discovering mineral wealth.

The conquest of the Indians and the search for minerals long preceded the arrival of Afonso Furtado in Brazil, but both processes were considerably intensified during his administration. The expansion of settlement and the opening of cattle ranges in the interior had brought the Portuguese into increasing and usually hostile contact with the Indians of the sertão. Some groups like the Aimoré of Ilhéus and Porto Seguro took the offensive and raided down to the coast, burning plantations and threatening towns. Although punitive expeditions led by local captains were dispatched, resistance continued. Indians attacked plantations in Capanema (1612); at Aporá (1621);[3] and at Itapororocas, Jaguaripe, Maragogipe, and Jiquiriça (1630s-40). In 1640 the decision was made to wage a general war against the uncontrolled tribes, but action was delayed by the war against the Dutch in Pernambuco (1645-54). Indian raids continued as did colonial counterattacks, like that led by Gaspar Dias Adorno in 1654. The following year peace with the Paiäiäs broke down and Tomé Dias Laços reduced them once again to colonial control. A military column sent to the mountains of Orobó established a fort for Indian control, but many soldiers died there from disease and the fort was abandoned.[4]

Incessant warfare and its disruptive effects on the economy of the northeast called for a new response. The Paulistas' reputation as Indian fighters and backwoodsmen was not lost on the colonists and administrators in the northeastern captaincies of Brazil. As early as 1657 royal officials considered using Paulista mercenaries, and in 1658 the Paulista Domingos Barbosa Calheiros led an expedition from Salvador to the region near Jacobina, raiding the villages of the Topinis and the Maracavaçús.[5] Barbosa Calheiros's effort had little success and over the next few years different tribes raided Cairú, Jiquiriça, and Itapororocas, where even the help of the now "tame" Paiäiäs could not save the ranches of João Peixoto Viegas, principal landowner in the district.[6] These actions disrupted the population and economy of Bahia. Many people fled to the Recôncavo to escape the Indian attacks, and the abandonment of some areas led to shortages in manioc flour and firewood, products of the interior crucial to the colony's sugar production. In 1669 new Indian attacks caused the governor, Alexandre de Sousa Freire, to convoke a general session of the High Court which resulted in a declaration of war against the tribes of the interior. Once again help was to be sought from the guerrilla fighters of São Paulo. Negotiations with wealthy Paulista Pedro Vaz broke down, but in his place two other Paulistas, Estevão Ribeiro Baião Parente and Bras Rodrigues Arzão, agreed to accept the challenge of a campaign in the Bahian backlands. Their arrival in the northeast marked the beginning of an epoch. From the 1670s to the mid-eighteenth century, groups of itinerant Paulistas could be found in the central and northeastern regions from Minas Gerais to Ceará, campaigning against escaped slaves and hostile Indians—and sometimes against peaceful settlers and friendly Indians as well, in their constant search for wealth, lands, and captives.

The activities of Estevão Ribeiro Baião Parente, his son João

Amaro, and the second-in-command, Bras Rodrigues Arzão, are well known. Scattered sources document the arrival of their troops in Bahia, their relatively unsuccessful first campaign along the Paraguaçu River, and their second entrada of 1672-73, which resulted in the capture of 1,500 Indians, half of whom died in the forced march back to Salvador.[7] Their expeditions and later activities resulted in the settlement of Camisão, Massacará, Maracás, and Santo Antônio da Conquista (later renamed João Amaro), all former Indian villages in the Bahian sertão, and opened up the sertão on both banks of the Paraguaçu River. The broad outlines of these campaigns are clear, but much detail is missing from the historical record. Afonso Furtado's letter to the town council of São Paulo describing the success of these bandeiras has been lost, as have most of the documents in the register of São Paulo's correspondence from 1672 to 1677. This lacuna has caused the principal historian of the bandeiras, Afonso de Escragnolle Taunay, to lament that he could find no new material on this expedition.[8] Lopes Sierra's manuscript demonstrates that in fact there were four entradas under Afonso Furtado, rather than the two mentioned in the traditional historiography. Moreover, it provides details concerning the routes of march and organization of the expeditions that can be found in no other source; therefore, the manuscript is an important addition to the literature on the *bandeirantes* as well as a new source on government and life in late seventeenth-century Brazil.

The second aspect of the penetration of the sertão, the search for mineral wealth, is a story as old as the presence of the Portuguese in Brazil. During the sixteenth century numerous expeditions set out in search of minerals, but despite occasional reports of strikes there was little result. Portuguese efforts intensified after 1545 when the great Spanish mine at Potosí in Upper Peru (modern Bolivia) revealed the existence of great riches on the continent. Portuguese colonists and administrators were sure that similar riches must also exist in their region of America. They were correct, as the gold and diamond strikes of the eighteenth century were to prove, but it took a century and a half of exploration, error, and false alarm before there were any positive discoveries.

The pace of exploration varied over time. In Bahia the search intensified from the 1580s to the 1620s, then seemed to decline as the sugar industry reached its zenith.[9] It would surge again only as the vicissitudes of agriculture became apparent by the 1670s. Still, throughout the seventeenth century, reports of diamonds, silver, gold, and emeralds filtered down to the coast, and more than one expedition had its hopes dashed when samples turned out to be not silver but malachite. However many the disappointments, the sertão remained a region of hope, promising fabled wealth to those willing to brave its dangers. By the end of the seventeenth century royal administrators were increasingly interested in supporting the search for minerals.

ECONOMIC CAUSES OF BRAZILIAN EXPANSION

Afonso Furtado has long appeared in Brazilian historiography as a man obsessed with the search for mines and mineral wealth. The origin of his interest in mines has often been sought in his own personality and proclivities. One distinguished historian calls him an "El Doradomaniac" and suggests that Afonso Furtado was so obsessed because he had a distant New Christian (converted Jewish) ancestor.[10] Despite these notions an important question remains: why did the search for mines play such an important role in Afonso Furtado's administration? Perhaps the answer is to be found not in the personality of Afonso Furtado, but in the changing economic structure of the Portuguese empire and in the critical position of the Brazilian economy within it.

For about a hundred years (1570-1670) Brazil dominated the European market for sugar. Plantations around Bahia and Pernambuco grew rapidly in the late sixteenth century, making use of rich soils, a favorable climate, and large numbers of Indian and

African slaves. By 1600 Brazil had about 200 plantations, or engenhos, producing over 8,400 tons of sugar a year. Prosperous times continued until the 1630s when the Dutch, as part of their struggle against the Spanish Hapsburgs, launched a major attack against the Portuguese empire—from 1580 to 1640 it was also under Hapsburg control.[11] The Dutch occupied Pernambuco and much of the northeastern coast of Brazil, and, although their goal was to continue sugar production, the fighting and the subsequent Luso-Dutch War (1645-54) disrupted the sugar economy. After the expulsion of the Dutch, the sugar economy recovered in the 1660s, but by that time international conditions had changed considerably. The Dutch and English had founded their own plantation colonies in the Caribbean and had established themselves on the African coast at the supply sources of the slave trade. Brazilian planters and Portuguese merchants experienced serious competition both in the European sugar market and for the supply of slaves. Prices for sugar began to fall while those for slaves began to rise. These problems, in addition to several poor harvests in Brazil and certain structural difficulties such as over-expansion within the industry, signaled increasingly hard times for the Brazilian colony. Many historians have dated the origins of this situation about the year 1670; thus Afonso Furtado was the first governor to face the crisis of late seventeenth-century Brazil.

We get some idea of the Brazilian perception of the crisis in a letter written to the crown in 1672 by the city council (*Câmara*) of Bahia. The council, generally representative of the interests of the sugar planters, complained about the many taxes levied on sugar, the high cost of supplies, the lack of slaves and the elevated prices for them, and especially the reluctance of merchants to buy Brazilian sugar because of its low price in European markets.[12] The Câmara repeated these complaints in 1673 and 1674 to Afonso Furtado, but he seems to have done little to alleviate the situation —nor, in fact, was there much that he could have done.[13] Between 1650 and 1668 the price of sugar had fallen from 3,800 *réis* for an *arroba* to 2,400 réis, a decline of 33 percent.[14] Brazil was a colony, and the key to the problem lay not so much in Brazil as in the Atlantic economy and Portugal's role within it.

For over a century and a half the Portuguese empire had depended on the valuable products of its overseas possessions and outposts to provide the economic resources of empire. Black pepper from Asia, black people from Africa, and white sugar from Brazil had brought the nations of Europe to Lisbon and had provided Portugal with goods to be traded for manufactures and for specie. The small amounts of gold that had come to Portugal from West Africa, India, and the mines of Monomotapa in East Africa were never enough to satisfy the need for specie. By the seventeenth century Portugal depended on its trade with Spain and those who traded with Spain for a supply of silver that Spain, in turn, acquired from its mines in Peru and Mexico. Brazilian sugar, dyewood, spices, and other commodities earned Portugal the specie and manufactured goods necessary to maintain its empire. The late seventeenth century created difficult times for Portugal, not only because the competition of other nations had reduced the buying power of Brazil's products, but also because of a crisis in silver production. The mines of Peru and Mexico were no longer producing at former levels, and Spain had less silver to pay for its exchanges. Portugal found its finances strained by the war against the Dutch (1645-54), the struggle for independence from Spain (1640-67), and other debts in Europe. The crown responded to this situation by devaluating its currency for the remainder of the century. Moreover, the new exclusivist mercantilism of Jean-Baptiste Colbert limited the market for Portuguese goods in France. Portugal found by 1670 that its colonial goods could no longer earn the specie and the manufactures that it needed. Lisbon responded with reforms and with its own Colbertianism, sponsoring by 1670 the creation of light industries that could provide some of the goods needed. This policy was interrupted in 1695 when gold was discovered in Brazil, and Portugal once again had all the hard currency it needed to buy whatever it desired elsewhere in Europe, at least temporarily.[15]

In Brazil, the period between 1670 and the discovery of gold in 1695 was marked by economic difficulty, crises in agriculture, and a new search for mineral wealth. From the time the colony was discovered, explorers, prospectors, and Indian hunters had searched for mines, which they were always sure lay beyond the next mountain range or across the next river.[16] Few had been found, and by 1600 the search for mines had decreased in intensity as the agricultural prosperity of the sugar plantations had increased. Brazil was often short of currency, but during the union with Spain an active, if sometimes illegal, commerce had developed between Brazil and Buenos Aires, where slaves and goods were traded for silver brought down from Potosí.[17] Pyrard de Laval, a French traveler to Bahia in 1610, was particularly impressed by the free circulation of Spanish silver in Brazil.[18] After the separation of Spain and Portugal in 1640, Brazil found this supply disrupted, which added to the difficulties of the sugar market and created by 1670 a critical situation in the colony. Portuguese efforts to discover new sources of mineral wealth were not limited to Brazil. In East Africa, the 1670s witnessed new attempts to tap the gold in the kingdom of Monomotapa (present-day Malawi) and in 1678 a silver expedition went up the Zambezi River but with little to show for the effort.[19] These activities, like the actions of Afonso Furtado in Brazil, were symptomatic of the economic situation of the Portuguese empire in the last decades of the seventeenth century.

Within this economic context the actions of Afonso Furtado and the activities that characterized Brazil in the late seventeenth century come sharply into focus. The period after 1670 was a time of widespread, new penetration into the Brazilian interior and renewed interest in the search for mineral wealth. Eliminating Indian groups in the sertão served a double purpose for the colony: it protected the plantations from Indian depredations and opened new areas for prospecting and cattle ranching. The latter activity was becoming important because of the active commerce in hides developing between Brazil and Portugal. The southern town of São Paulo, long a staging center for such exploring and slave-hunting forays, began to send out expeditions with renewed vigor. Some of these moved northward into the area that later became Minas Gerais, the zone of the great gold strike of 1695; others moved onto the plains of the south. The establishment in 1680 of a Portuguese outpost at Colônia do Sacramento on the north bank of the Rio de la Plata represented a desire not only to open the ranges in the south but to reopen trade with Spanish America and its silver.[20] New sources of wealth preoccupied the governors of Brazil, for they seemed to be a remedy for the ills of both colony and metropolis. That preoccupation became clear in the government of Afonso Furtado.

THE HERO: AFONSO FURTADO DE CASTRO DO RIO DE MENDONÇA

The social ascendancy of Afonso Furtado was relatively recent, as such matters were measured in Portugal. His family's nobility was based on a grant by the king, Dom Sebastião, in 1571 to Diogo de Castro do Rio in recognition of services in India, Africa, and Portugal.[21] The family's fortunes were advanced when in 1575 Diogo de Castro do Rio purchased the lands of Barbacena near the city of Elvas in Alentejo province. The purchase included the rights of lordship over the town of Barbacena and its inhabitants. These estates, purchased by Afonso Furtado's great-grandfather, were legally established as an entail (*morgado*) and became the family seat. It was probably here that Afonso Furtado was born in 1625 or 1626,[22] the only son among the four children of Dom Jorge Furtado de Mendonça.

When in 1640 João, duke of Bragança, initiated his movement for Portuguese independence from rule by the Hapsburg monarchs of Spain, the young Afonso Furtado cast his fortunes with the Bragança cause. Almost immediately he received authorization to enter the knightly Order of Christ and soon thereafter was serving in frontier campaigns against the Castilians.[23] His military career was excellent and he distinguished himself both on the battlefield and in the council chamber.

Afonso Furtado enters the historical record of the Wars of Restoration in 1652 as colonel of foot and governor of the town of Campo Mayor. He remained in the post five years, serving with his troops in a number of engagements in the vicinity. In 1657 he was promoted to the rank of general of artillery in Alentejo and from that point on began to figure prominently in the progress of the war.[24] He was at the relief of Olivença, and at the siege of Mourão he exposed himself to enemy fire while directing the successful attack. He and his family suffered a considerable loss when the Spaniards burned the town of Barbacena in 1658, but his military career continued at the same pace.[25] In 1659 he became general of the cavalry in Alentejo and in 1663 he was sent to govern the city of Estremoz. After the fall of Evora to the Spaniards, he joined in the battle to retake it. During the major Portuguese victory at Ameixal (June 8, 1663), he was in the first line of combat and had a horse shot out from under him.[26] The list of his campaign services contains the major engagements of the war, including a number of important victories in Spain. During 1665 he directed the siege of Zarza and the sack of Ferrera. His cavalry conducted a lightning strike across the border, capturing needed supplies and horses. In this campaign he was aided by his eldest son, Jorge Furtado de Mendonça, a commander of cavalry, and by his other son, João Furtado, who served as captain of his father's guard.[27]

For four years Afonso Furtado served as military governor of the province of Beira, and his reputation as a valorous and intelligent soldier was well established. In 1670 his letter of appointment as governor of Brazil noted that "to his valor and council a good part of the success of victories [was] owed."[28] He sailed for Brazil March 6, 1671, and despite a perilous voyage in which his ship was separated from the rest of the fleet, he arrived safely. A contemporary noted that Afonso Furtado had faced the perils of the sea with the same valor that he had faced those of the land. He was a man who was "as feared by his enemies as he was esteemed by his friends."[29]

But beneath the praise and the undeniable record of military achievement are shadows cast by controversy and dissatisfaction. The Brazilian historian Sebastião da Rocha Pitta wrote that Afonso Furtado was more "valourous than fortunate."[30] During the War of Restoration, he was satirized by the phrase "no intente el que no es dichoso" (the unlucky should not try).[31] This remark apparently referred to several unsuccessful military engagements including his failure to lift the siege of Olivença. His attack on a Castilian stronghold following the battle of Elvas was repulsed with heavy losses. Some, including the count of Ericeira, the major chronicler of the war, thought the attack unnecessary since the garrison surrendered on the following day when their reinforcement failed to arrive.[32] Although Afonso Furtado eventually received the title of viscount of Barbacena in 1671, he never referred to himself as such because he believed the title was not a sufficient recognition of his services.[33] It is tempting to speculate that his active direction of military campaigns and mineral exploration in Brazil was in some part motivated by a desire to reaffirm his merits and his claim to the title of count.

Aside from the details of his distinguished military career it is difficult to establish much about Afonso Furtado's personal life. In many ways he seems quite typical of Portuguese nobility in the Restoration period. In addition to the family entail of Barbacena, Afonso Furtado also acquired revenue-earning commanderies (*comendas*) as a member of the Order of Christ.[34] The chancellery registers of Dom Afonso VI are dotted with various pensions and loans extended to him by the crown.[35] Royal recognition came in December 1671, when he was granted the title of viscount of Barbacena, an honor rewarding his former military service and probably granted because of his willingness to serve in Brazil.[36]

As was customary for Portuguese overseas governors in the seventeenth century, Afonso Furtado was accompanied to Brazil by a retinue of relatives and retainers, foremost of whom were his younger son, João Furtado de Mendonça, and his nephew Antônio de Sousa e Meneses. His wife, Dona María de Távora, who was his cousin and the daughter of a former governor of Angola, remained in Portugal as did his elder son and heir, Jorge Furtado de Mendonça.[37] A daughter, Dona Magdalena, had entered a convent. Although the Lopes Sierra manuscript emphasizes Afonso Furtado's selfless administration, the governor, like most officials of his age, was not above providing for his own. Both his son and nephew received land grants in Bahia and military commissions. João Furtado also received a stipend from the Overseas Council that enabled him to bid for the whaling monopoly contract in Bahia.[38] While in Brazil, Afonso Furtado did not forget his family fortunes in Portugal, receiving in 1672 the right to pass his title of viscount to his elder son.[39] Despite the usual opportunities of malfeasance, Afonso Furtado died in Brazil indebted, and only a plea from his widow and heirs to the Overseas Council in Lisbon resulted in the government's liquidation of his debts.[40]

The manuscript published here is primarily a defense of Afonso Furtado's administration, and except for his religiosity it reveals very little about the man—his personality and private life. In truth, the documentary record in this regard is slim, but the governor's official correspondence does, from time to time, cast light on these matters. Afonso Furtado was by training and experience a soldier, and his government reflected a soldier's concerns: loyalty, the chain of command, and the obedience of inferiors. Before his appointment in Brazil his governing experience had been in military posts during the War of Restoration in Portugal. When the war ended he was one of a generation of soldiers called into royal bureaucratic service, especially in colonial posts.[41] Afonso Furtado's model of government was always that of the battlefield. When he arrived in Brazil in 1671, his first actions were to review the state of the defenses and the condition and strength of the troops. Lopes Sierra's manuscript concentrates on Afonso Furtado's direction of successful campaigns against the Indians of Bahia, and it is obvious from the emphasis placed upon this aspect of his government that he took great pride in organizing and directing military campaigns.[42] On the eve of his death he also began to take an interest in suppressing the community of escaped slaves at Palmares, but its final destruction fell to his successors.[43]

Loyalty to his sovereign and a strict adherence to the hierarchy of authority emerge continually in Afonso Furtado's correspondence as his primary principles of government. He reprimanded the town council of Porto Seguro on one occasion, pointing out that "the service of His Highness is the first obligation to which everyone should attend"; in another instance, after threatening a subordinate with removal, he cajoled him as "such a good servant of His Highness" to act properly.[44] The loyalty that all owed the king was simply an extension of the deference that inferiors owed superiors. Because Afonso Furtado was jealous of his prerogatives of command as governor of Brazil, the continual restiveness of minor officials and the administrative conflicts that characterized so much of Brazil's colonial history must have caused him much aggravation. In 1672, for example, he reprimanded the governor of Pernambuco in the following manner: "Your Lordship cannot deny that you are a subject of this Government and that subjects even if they have much justice in their position should not defend their opinions but obey the orders of their superiors, and if they are unjust then the Prince will punish them."[45] This principle was stated even more clearly when he wrote in 1674 that "neither peoples nor inferior officers can resolve by themselves anything against the wishes of their superiors."[46] Despite Lopes Sierra's image of Afonso Furtado as a man who constantly sought advice from others, there is no question that he had a soldier's concept of authority and rule and brooked no questioning from subordinates.

Whatever his principles of government, Afonso Furtado brought with him Portuguese social attitudes that reflected the prevailing opinions of the nobility and were in many instances shared by the Brazilian colonists. He demonstrated very little sympathy for the Indians who endangered the colony and hindered its expansion.

Despite the fact that his instructions specifically ordered him to use peaceful means to secure the conversion of the gentiles, "the principal reason for our settlement of Brazil," he rather quickly assumed the prevailing attitudes of dislike and indifference held by most of the colonists. Like them, he generally referred to unconquered tribes as "barbarian gentiles," and he tended to define the Indian "problem" in strictly military terms.[47]

These attitudes were drawn sharply into focus in 1679 when the settlers of Maragogipe petitioned for the right to conquer Indians in the vicinity as they had done in the time of Afonso Furtado. To his credit, the governor at the time, Roque da Costa Barreto, objected. He stated that these Indians had simply defended themselves and their liberty in "natural and necessary defense" against those who sought to enslave them. It is not surprising that the Overseas Council in Lisbon overrode Costa Barreto because of the importance of this matter and because "of the inconstant nature of these barbarians."[48] Only Salvador de Sá, an old Brazil-hand himself, warned in council that such policies would eventually depopulate Brazil or turn the colony into another Chile, where a standing army was needed to control the Indians. Unfortunately, such attitudes were uncommon and most administrators in Portugal and colonists in Brazil supported the policies of conquest advocated by Afonso Furtado.

Afonso Furtado's attitudes toward Indians were paralleled by his perception of blacks. Noticeably absent from Lopes Sierra's panegyric are references to blacks or slaves—a rather striking omission since African slaves probably comprised 60 percent of the colony's population during the period. During his administration, Afonso Furtado did concern himself with some of the problems of a slave-based society. He maintained a lively correspondence with his subordinate Dom Pedro de Almeida, governor of Pernambuco, suggesting ways in which his campaigns against Indians in Bahia might provide examples for destroying the large community of escaped slaves at Palmares. He did offer a soldier's admiration for the former slaves' military capacities since "Palmares has resisted such good soldiers and such considerable forces that have gone against it on numerous occasions"; but, in general, he viewed the central problem once again as a military matter.[49] It is interesting to note that bush fighters from São Paulo were eventually used to destroy Palmares just as Afonso Furtado had used them against the Indians of Bahia.[50]

One incident is particularly revealing of Afonso Furtado's attitude toward Africans, a sentiment that he surely shared with most colonists in Brazil. In 1673 the governor of Angola sent several African princes to Brazil who would proceed from there to Lisbon as part of a quasi-diplomatic mission. Not only was Afonso Furtado reluctant to accept them, warning of dire consequences if they "escaped" and joined with fugitive slaves, but in his letter of receipt he made the following slip: "I received six *slaves* [italics added], I mean, six black princes . . . to be sent to the secretary of the Overseas Council."[51]

Despite the euologies of Juan Lopes Sierra, Afonso Furtado's administration was not particularly distinguished nor was his personality or background much different from that of most other Portuguese colonial governors of the period. His service in Brazil, like his military career, was marked by some successes and some notable disappointments, such as the failure to discover mineral wealth. Twenty years would pass before rumors of precious metals in Brazil would become reality.

THE MANUSCRIPT AS A HISTORICAL AND CULTURAL DOCUMENT

Since the nineteenth century, Brazilian and foreign scholars have searched the archives and libraries of Europe for sources that document Brazil's past. Their tireless efforts have revealed a vast corpus of historical materials and the quest is by no means over. What is surprising, however, is that important sources long known to scholars have sometimes gone unnoticed or unstudied. The "Paneguirico funebre" falls into that category. Scholars have been aware of the existence of Juan Lopes Sierra's biography of Afonso Furtado since the publication in 1946 of Carlos Alberto Ferreira's catalog of manuscripts relating to Brazil in the collection of the Biblioteca da Ajuda of Lisbon.[52] Despite the revelation of its existence, no historians of Brazil have used the "Paneguirico funebre" in any significant way. Nor is it the only work of this genre that has escaped the attention of scholars. The National Library of Lisbon, for example, houses a manuscript by Antônio Marquês de Perada, a long honorific biography of the Marquês das Minas, governor of Brazil (1683-87).[53] It too has never been used by modern historians of Brazil. Panegyric biographies and funeral orations form a literature that has not usually drawn the attention of historians of Portugal and colonial Brazil.[54] Reasons for the oversight are to some extent explained by the genre itself. Like most elegiac poetry of the seventeenth and eighteenth centuries, these works usually are poor literature. They are filled with hyperbole and badly constructed allegory and motivated not by profound sentiments of loss at the death of the subject, but by the author's desire for reward or patronage — art in the service of politics and pride.[55] Certainly Lopes Sierra's work, dedicated to Antônio de Sousa e Meneses, nephew of the deceased governor, indicates such a purpose. Yet, despite mundane motives of authorship and literary limitations, the "Paneguirico funebre" has value as a cultural and historical document, although this value must be understood within the context of the genre and the author's purpose.

As a history, the work presented here has severe limitations. Although the Lopes Sierra manuscript reveals details of many important aspects of Afonso Furtado's administration, the reader should be aware that it is not a comprehensive account of the governor's actions nor a history of Brazil or even of Bahia in this period. For example, the manuscript contains virtually nothing on agriculture, even though Brazil was at this time primarily an exporter of tropical crops and was, in fact, entering into a difficult phase in its agrarian development. This omission seems to be explained by

Afonso Furtado's lack of interest in the internal problems of export agriculture. The governor's responsibility to preside over and control the Royal High Court (*Relação*) also receives scant notice, even though the actions and excesses of judges plagued Bahia. Brazilian-born magistrate Cristovão de Burgos had become wealthy and powerful, and his refusal to pay taxes, emulated by other judges, became a major cause for local complaint.[56] These problems, coupled with claims that justice was being sold to the highest bidder, led the crown in 1673 to order Afonso Furtado to investigate. The author mentions neither the problem nor the actions of the governor.

Instead, the manuscript emphasizes two areas of activity: Indian campaigns and the search for mines. But, even here, the record is incomplete. There are no references to the campaign mounted against the Galachos, who raided along the São Francisco River in 1673 and against whom the Bahian landowner Francisco Dias d'Avila and the Paulistas had battled.[57] More important is the absence of any mention of Afonso Furtado's contact in 1672 with Fernão Dias Pais. Dias Pais, a famous Paulista backwoodsman, was commissioned to search for the fabled mountain of emeralds, with the mellifluous name Sabarabuçu, in the region of Espirito Santo and Minas Gerais.[58] This expedition was the second part of a two-pronged effort to discover mineral wealth in Brazil; the first part, the efforts of Don Rodrigo de Castelo Branco to find silver mines, is detailed in Lopes Sierra's manuscript. Both searches proved fruitless, but the author's failure to mention the activities of Dias Pais underlines both the incomplete nature of the manuscript as a history of the period and the fact that the author seems to have concentrated his attention on those people and events that he, as a resident in Salvador, personally knew or witnessed. Thus, as an account of Afonso Furtado's administration, the manuscript is selective and very much oriented toward events in the colonial capital of Salvador and its region.

Although there are real deficiencies in the historical record presented in the "Paneguirico funebre," Lopes Sierra compensates with a detailed description of the death and funeral of Afonso Furtado. In the texture of its presentation and in the events it details, the description reveals the concerns and style of a colonial society in the baroque age. As a colony of Portugal, Brazil was profoundly influenced by post-Tridentine Catholicism, a reaction to the rationalism of the Renaissance and the subsequent critiques of humanists and schismatics. Although much has been written about the late baroque culture of eighteenth-century Minas Gerais, little attention has been given to the early manifestations of this manner of thought and life in the coastal cities of Brazil.[59] Salvador was, and is, a city of religions. Construction of many of its churches began in the decades just before 1670, a result of the convergence of high times for the sugar industry and a deepening religiosity. The luxurious ornamentation of the Jesuit school, the Church of the Misericórdia, and the convent of São Francisco are artifacts of the style and piety of the period. That it was a piety often corrupted by power and profligacy, as we learn from authors like Father Antônio Vieira and Gregório de Matos, need not concern us here.[60] The baroque style in art and life was the reaffirmation of basic cultural values and ideals in which Catholicism of the Counter-Reformation was a central element.

No event so suited an author in the baroque tradition as the death of a high public official. Death itself served as a symbol of passage and a mystical reaffirmation of Divine Force. Death and the funeral were acts of theater. The pomp and ceremony permitted a display of the power and union of church and state, as Lopes Sierra makes clear in his description of the participation of various religious, civil, and military dignitaries. Although it is the elite that takes the active role, the funeral is a popular event, popular in the sense that it is a spectacle designed for the consumption and edification of the populace. The richly adorned funeral bier, the military regalia, the colors and decorative details, and the apparent miracles and signs of divine grace are all embellishments on the basic rites of the Church.[61] Lopes Sierra's emphasis on the visual impact of these elements is characteristic of baroque literature, and the elements themselves reveal the central concerns and ethos of this society. To the modern reader the painstaking attention to artistic and decorative detail, and the long description of the ceremonies surrounding the interment, may seem tedious and unnecessary. If, however, they are viewed as both a typical literary device of that age and an accurate portrayal of the essential ideological and political concerns of Brazilian society in the late seventeenth century, the value becomes apparent. The "Paneguirico funebre" documents not only a governor's administration, but also the style and culture of an Iberian colony in the baroque age.[62]

THE AUTHOR:
JUAN LOPES SIERRA

In Salvador the real and allegorical distance between the imposing churches and the bustling wharves of the sugar warehouses was slight. Concern for the sublime themes of a profound Christianity and the mundane concerns of wealth, sex, and scandal created a milieu for intense literary activity. Salvador in the late seventeenth century was filled with poets and writers of widely varying literary talent. One of the period's two dominant figures was the Jesuit preacher and master of the Portuguese language, Father Antônio Vieira, whose pen was often a tool of social criticism. The other (at least in the quality of the work produced) was satiric poet-lawyer Gregório de Matos e Guerra,[63] who criticized the social and political life of the colony and the foibles of the governors and the governed. Others produced less notable accomplishments. Men like Gonçalo Soares de França, Manuel Botelho de Oliveira, and the secretary of state, Bernardo Vieira Ravasco, were all part of a flourishing Bahian literary community.[64] The intense literary activity is somewhat surprising since no printing press existed in Brazil at this time and thus many works were never published. Still, the authors of Bahia produced sonnets, sermons, letters, and satiric poetry. It is in the context of this literary activity that Juan Lopes Sierra's work must be understood.

Lopes Sierra, author of the "Paneguirico funebre," is a mysterious figure about whom virtually nothing is known except for the information he provides about himself in this work. Since he informs the reader that he was seventy-two when the work was completed (1676), we can place his birth at c. 1604. The place of birth remains unknown, although the language of the text and his difficulty with Portuguese proper names and orthography indicate that he was a Spaniard. What this Spaniard was doing in Brazil during a period of hostilities between Portugal and Spain is a question that cannot be answered at present. Although he claimed to have written twenty-five other works, except for the *Antecatastrophe* fragment there is no reference to him in the guides to Iberian bibliography. This is not surprising since the works of many authors, like Gregório de Matos, circulated only in manuscript. A search through the royal chancellery books in Lisbon failed to reveal any appointment or stipend awarded to him by the crown, indicating that he held no office. His own failure to mention any ecclesiastical affiliation seems to preclude his membership in the clergy.

Lopes Sierra refers to himself as "The Rustic." He claims to have had only nine months of formal schooling. Although his use of "The Rustic" may be only a baroque conceit, his common errors of orthography and the seeming lack of polish in the work would indicate a limited literary background. He does draw on both the Old and New Testaments and on classical authors, especially the historians Herodotus, Livy, and perhaps Plutarch, but his knowledge of these sources is superficial. We may, in fact, be dealing with a self-taught author.

Little can be learned of the author's life from the manuscript. We find that Lopes Sierra was in Granada in 1621 (p. 52, this volume) and in Seville in 1625 (p. 82). The date of his arrival in Brazil and the reasons for it remain obscure. Many Spaniards did go to Brazil during the Iberian union (1580-1640) when Spain and

Portugal shared monarchs. Aside from immigrants and merchants, large contingents of Castilian and Neapolitan troops also served in Brazil during the war against the Dutch. Perhaps Lopes Sierra was among those few who chose to recognize the Bragança cause and to remain in the colony after 1640.

Most curious of all are Lopes Sierra's references in the "Paneguirico funebre" to knowing and conversing with figures such as distinguished Jesuit Father Simão de Vasconcelos; Don Rodrigo de Castelo Branco; Portuguese soldier and author Francisco Manuel de Mello; secretary of state for Brazil, Bernardo Vieira Ravasco; and others prominent in the social and religious life of Bahia. He claims at one point to have conversed personally with the king, Dom João IV (p. 150). Such associations and contacts would indicate a man of status and importance, the sort of individual bound to appear in coeval documentation. But the record is virtually silent. Lopes Sierra is not listed as a brother of the socially prominent Misericórdia, Bahia's major charitable institution, nor does his name appear in the records of the municipal council of Salvador. And, as indicated earlier, the chancellery records contain no reference to him. In fact, in neither Portugal nor Brazil have materials appeared that might provide information on his life.

Of course, it is possible that Lopes Sierra was an imposter, an *embusteiro*, a literary hack who by name-dropping, false claims, and self-promotion hoped to ingratiate himself with some powerful or wealthy patron. Honorific biographies and funeral euologies were perfect genres for the purposes of such individuals, and in the history of the Portuguese empire, enough examples exist of these literary sycophants. We know from the author's own statement that the idea of the "Paneguirico funebre" was born in an audience with Antônio de Sousa e Meneses, the governor's nephew, who made a request that led Lopes Sierra to undertake this tribute.

Finally, we must consider the possibility that "Juan Lopes Sierra" is a pseudonym. Gregório de Matos, Manuel Botelho de Oliveira, and many if not most of the Bahian literati of the period were capable of writing in Spanish. The fact that Afonso Furtado's administration was a controversial one could have led an author to seek anonymity. Still, the particularly poor orthography of Portuguese and Brazilian place-names argues against this, indicating instead that the author was not born in Brazil and that Portuguese was not his native tongue. More important, there exists what appears to be a single set of contemporaneous references to the author. A letter from the count of Atouguia, governor of Brazil (1654-57), to the municipal council of Salvador, notes the petition of a "João Lopes Serra" who was seeking a patent for a new way to make sugar with less firewood.[65] This and the council's discussion are the only independent references yet discovered to the mysterious author of the "Paneguirico funebre."[66]

LIFE or FUNEREAL EULOGY

to Afonso Furtado de Castro do Rio de Mendonça, Viscount of Barbacena, Constable-major of Covilhã, Commander of the estates of São Julião de Bragança, São Romão de Fonte Coberta and São João de Refriegas, [member] of the Order of Christ, Governor and Captain General of the land and sea of this state of Brazil

and

DEDICATED

to Antônio de Sousa e Meneses, Commander of the Habit of Christ

and [written]

by a rustic in the sciences, Juan Lopes Sierra

1676

City of São Salvador Bahia de Todos os Santos, Brazil

DEDICATORY LETTER

to

Antônio de Sousa e Meneses

No prerogative, Sir, so eulogizes princes as the ability of benevolent ones to tolerate easy confidences. Alexander, as emperor, was so severe in his benevolence that when his mother, Mamea, censured him, he answered, "No one, Madam, should leave the presence of the emperor discontent." Your Grace, may God protect you, is one of these. Not only by reason of your own generosity, but also owing to the generous blood of the Sousas and Meneses, you did not want me to leave your presence [discontent] that day, when, tendering my sorrow at the death of your uncle, I, being unlettered, was quick to offer you that which wise and learned men disavow. And with reason, for those who know how to publish perfect eulogies are few. But Your Grace not only did not reject my indiscreet confidence and easy offer, but thanked me for my intent, a favor that so obligated me that I immediately took up my pen.

I thought, Sir, that upon embarking on such a sublime task my pen would finish it quickly. But instead of flying across the paper it was slower than an ox. Astonished at its sloth, I inquired as to the cause and discovered that the barnacle delaying it was a statement made by Memory. It demonstrated precisely the paucity of my ability and the importance of a task that even for the wealthy [and schooled] would be difficult. Instead of being hurt I [realized] I deserved not only what it was saying but also the fact that it had stopped my pen, and thus I told it:

"You are foolish, Memory. Fortunately my judgment ignores what you are repeating to my pen. No. You know who encourages its boldness. Be advised that princes appreciate simple goodwill more than rhetorical and silvered eloquences, for the latter include adulation and the former shows a guileless spirit. Xerxes demonstrated this clearly when he showed more appreciation for the humble present of the rustic than for great gifts of princes.[1]

"No one can be assured, O Memory, that I shall write in the manner and with the dignity of Homer or Vergil, because they know that I cannot. But what can be expected of me is a plain song from my flute or clumsy pen, leaving for the learned men the harmony of their lyres."

And thus Memory was silenced, and my pen, if it did not fly to the region of such a sublime sphere, at least executed all that my love and goodwill could direct. And because Your Grace was kind enough to admire the offer in flower, so should you accept the fruit, for you may rest assured that no one, seeing it [protected] under such generous wings, will dare offend it, just as there was no one who censured the confidence of the rustic upon seeing the acceptance of Xerxes. May God keep your [august] person. The fifteenth of February, 1676.

The servant of Your Grace,

uan Lopes sierra

PROLOGUE

*J*udgment does not always work with what it knows and what it understands, discreet friend and reader. Sometimes, many times, it gives in to the will of its whims. Mine, although unschooled, did not ignore the fact that it was incapable of such a great task. In addition, there was no dearth of letters to advise me that, of the twenty-five works I had written, this was the greatest I had undertaken. Forced to admit the justification of their arguments, I could not let that which merited diamond-point engraving pass in silence. And so I said to myself, "Let us begin. Although my work may not be a clock that all heed because of the accuracy of its hours, it will serve in the blackness of its lines if not in its voice, which is poorly articulated for lack of science." For just as in black and rough stones one can find veins of gold, silver, and diamonds, so also the deeds and sayings of our hero are gems that will shine through the crude words of my pen. He who looks for pearls must first search the rough shells before finding them. He who looks for gold and silver must first open the mine with hard iron before finding its treasure.

So you, friend and reader, should understand that if you do not labor in examining the rustic pages of this report, you will not find the precious pearls of the sayings of our hero; and if the hard iron of your attention does not penetrate the essence of his soul, you will not realize the richness with which his deeds are filled.

I hope to give them to you well-seasoned—although I am not a skilled chef—so that they will not bore you. In the historical events you will find entertainment; in the sayings and deeds of our hero, a lesson for the soul and for the body: a new thing, indeed something novel, to find in a secular man of these times. I shall not sell him to you as a saint, but weigh his life and death with that of others in whom diverse obligations concur, and you will see how your scales balance.

I say to you again that in the deeds and sayings of our hero, you will find enough material for your entertainment, because of their grandeur and of the many and beautiful forms and figures they take.

Look at them carefully and weigh them on the scales of your reason. Your faithful servant will tell them to you not in the showy lines of a mute clock but in clear accents such as those heard in the sonorous echoes of a bell. Hear them and you will discover what the great Afonso Furtado de Castro do Rio de Mendonça said. He is the master of my endeavor and of all you see written [here] in unschooled lines by a rustic. God has given order to this world and promontory of planets and stars. Your faithful servant will demonstrate this, using the weight of reason which, when weighed and not [allowed to] wander, [will show] the instability of the stars and planets and the firmness of this world.

I shall end by saying that the love and goodwill I had for this famous hero, more than my capability, obliges me to take up my pen and serves as my excuse. I am censured in that I do not write correctly, that I lack letters, and that my spelling is poor. I admit these faults and submit two reasons for them. The first is that I studied the ABCs for only nine months. The second is that I am writing this by my own hand at the age of seventy-two.[2]

FUNEREAL EULOGY
to the honor of
Afonso Furtado de Castro
do Rio de Mendonça
Governor and Captain General
of This State of Brazil

Noble Brazilians, to whom are owed with reason greater applause than those which one unschooled in the sciences can communicate to you, hear, hear and you will see how much more properly I take license when I now try to write a statement for you than did the apostle Saint Paul when he wrote to the Romans. He told them, "Romans, Romans, it is not that I am ignorant of your understanding, but only that I want to refresh your memory." I say the same to you, noble ecclesiastics, distinguished secular gentlemen, royal magistrates of justice, gentlemen and good men of this city. My account consists not of rhetorical figures with which the ingenious poet or eloquent orator embellishes his stories and histories, a thing that [I], a rustic, cannot do.

I offer you the naked truth easily seen by your eyes, easily heard by your ears, not in speculative ideas but in clearly understood language. I do this by reason of seeing how rightly you showed yourselves bereaved for having lost that laurel which crowned the heroic head of whom you were the body, that which conserved you in peace and justice and which knew, as Sebola who liberated Rome from the tyrannical yoke, [how] to liberate your country from the indomitable barbarian.[3]

In its pages you will find, although in rough outline, the most famous hero seen by the ages whether in life or in death, a man whose greatest epitaph is to be called a man. And rightly so, for we know that when God wanted to make an image in His likeness, He did not say let us create an angel or an armed seraph, nor less that luminous torch that alights the planets and stars, but let us create man, an emblem in which He delineated His ultimate and absolute wisdom.

The deeds and sayings of this gallant hero will show you this truth, when you know that in twenty-eight years of martial treaties, battles, and encounters with the powerful arms of the Lion of Spain, he was never conquered but always the victor. If he was a Viriato in war, in peace he was not one but two Alexanders, The Severe in justice and The Great in generosity.[4]

But where, where are you taking me, Memory, through such humble passages to describe a hero such as the ages never have seen nor have the histories described. Let the resounding trumpet celebrate the news of his fame as it can the deeds of his life, but not [the news] of his death. Let Plutarch relate the illustrious victories of Alexander against princes and monarchs; he will not relate the victory of his death, for it was a poison that triumphed over his vigorous years.

Let them celebrate the deeds of Julius Caesar and say that he was the first emperor of Rome; but they will not celebrate his death, for the knife blows were those of Brutus and Cassius.

Let it be celebrated that the famous Hannibal had triumphed so many times against the eagles of Rome; but they cannot celebrate his death, for he took poison by his own hands, while the hands of our hero, at the time of his death, clasped tightly those hands that would lead him to eternal life.

All of this you will confess when the words and deeds of this valiant hero become clear through these black lines as the planets and stars let themselves be seen in the darkening shadows. But much better still when you see them arranged by a cultured and able gardener, not in rustic concepts but in candid and classical opinions that a learned mind, like a perennial fountain, is able to administer much better than I. I do no more than follow the steps of one who sows wheat, who unites in byways that which he finds divided, letting a more worthy gardener divide the straw from his beautiful grain.

Thus, with the force of my pen, I shall go forward uniting the words and deeds that this excellent man wrought in the government of this state in four years, six months, and twenty days, so that they may be perceived not like those of a crow, as mine are, but as those of an eagle, and they may rise to that sphere where one would fly to examine the most flaming rays of the sun.

Such a great subject really requires a Homer or a Vergil to recount it, but for the lack of such a worthy pen, no other eloquence suffices but his excellent words, which are such that without art of science they can be seen positioned in this star-studded globe so that as [the stars] they will never be found outside their sphere.

The agent for such a notorious function will be the resounding voice of fame that will travel from sunrise to sunset, publicizing his words to all it meets and seeing them reborn each day at the break of dawn. All this is deserved by one who discovered how to conquer, like that so valiant and spirited figure who dared to match lances with the lord of his estate in the Damascene field.

Know, know, O distinguished Brazilians, that the touchstone that marks the carats of the great heroes is death. This is what a phantom voice said to Charles V, the emperor, seeing him glorifying himself because of his triumphs and victories. "Charles, Charles," it said, "your vanity is deceiving you. The greatest deed is to know how to die."

But before that, the wise man Solon related this to King Croesus, called The Rich. He found him, one day, filled with glories and rich with trophies, believing that no one on the face of the earth was more fortunate than he. Wanting to be told so by another, he called the wise man Solon to him. When Solon arrived, he told him of his good fortunes and asked if he had ever seen a more fortunate man in the world than he. "In Athens," he answered, "I saw a man named Telon who, because of his good life and death, could be called fortunate."

And asking if he had seen others: "In the city of Argos," he answered, "I saw two brothers, one called Cleobis, the other Biton, who lived and died in such a way that they were also given the titles of fortunate."

Angry, the king asked him, "And me, in what place do you put me?" "A rich man," he said, "but fortunate, no, for this title is only given to those who experience a good death." And this must be why Augustus Caesar, when dying, asked his soldiers if he had played his role well in life, supposing that as one's life was, so would be one's death. The words and deeds of our hero will tell of his.[5]

This brief introduction will serve as an index to show us, as the clock gives the course of the hours, the words and deeds of our hero in the four years, six months, and twenty days that lapsed from the seventh of May, 1671, until the twenty-sixth of November, 1675. First, we shall describe the conditions of the land: a canvas on which the lines of his resolutions are to be fixed.

Government of Alexandre de Sousa [Freire], year 1671

Peace between Portugal and Spain

War is the plague of the poor

This state was governed by Alexandre de Sousa [Freire], as illustrious by his blood as worthy of such an honorific position.[6] Not many months had passed after his arrival when His Highness, may God keep him, made known the treaty of peace between that country and the Spanish crown—a day full of joy for the subjects of both realms, and rightly so, for war is like a disease-laden breeze that infects the powerful and arrogant, and the most humble pay for its damages.[7]

But, as it is natural that the times be inconsistent, another event followed that joyous news which not only was not joyous but caused not a little consternation. And it was to advise His Highness to do everything possible for the defense of this town, both in its fortifications and in arms and soldiers, because there was news that in Holland an armada was being prepared to set forth.

News of an enemy armada

This news came to the governor while he was sick in bed, and it vexed him greatly, for the fortifications were made of earth and the weather was such that it could dissolve even stones. In truth, they were in such a state that the principal ones needed much work, and the smaller ones—for example, the fort of Santo Antonio to the northeast—needed to be saved from ruin. That one did not even have gun carriages, nor the redoubts and platforms capable of holding artillery; it lacked arms, and those it did have were corroded from the disuse of peace.

State of this town with respect to arms

But the great care and vigilance of the governor was such that this was taken care of and remedies were hastily executed. Not much later the viceroy of India, Antônio de Melo e Castro, arrived from there.[8] Upon arriving, the order of His Highness was made known to him, and he and his son came to the palace to present themselves as if they were officials and to receive the orders of the governor, which, when given, referred to the rebuilding of the fortresses by the engineers. When the approaches to the city were secured with trenches and other works, it was seen how important in similar cases it

The viceroy of India, Antônio de Melo e Castro, fortifies the fortresses

was to have a good leader; for as an example that the soldiers might see, he was the first to take up the shovel and the pick. No one remained who did not work—just as with parts of the human body, the feet do what the head commands.

Four colonels are named and four companies of cavalry are formed

It was ordered that there be four colonels and that these lead from their regions the captains with all their men. The same was done with the southern towns, the city of Sergipe de El-Rey, which is fifty leagues from here, having formed from its region four companies of cavalry whose captains were noble gentlemen.[9]

The settlers dress up to wait for the enemy

This was the first order of His Highness to these his vassals. As a demonstration of their goodwill, they all came dressed in their very best according to rank, a voluntary action taken by those who like to carry out what the will demands. And so the countryside and the city became a veritable springtime of colors.

The arms furnished, the fortifications rebuilt, shot and powder replenished, the people brought in from all parts, everything was readied, with the colonels marching to the palace in the vanguard, and the two field masters of the paid regiments in the rear. And let it be understood that the enemy did not appear, and everyone was ordered to return to his home, something that calmed the populace even though they regretted the expenses incurred.

Rebellion of the city of Sergipe de El-Rey

Not long after this, the city of Sergipe de El-Rey rebelled against its captain major, and not only that, it took up arms to oppose the orders of its captain general, a fact that caused the infantry to be ordered out to suppress the rebellion.

Following this civil case was one of greater magnitude, involving more people. It was this: the barbarians had come to overrun the settlers of the mountain range, stretching from the north to the south in the western part, and the southern villages: Cairú, Camamú, Ilhéus, Jaguaripe, Cachoeira, Capanema, and Paraguaçu. Killing and robbing in such a depraved and resolute manner, they even searched out the captains of the infantry who were in the different areas and [were] trying to evade them. They killed Captain Manoel Barbosa.[10]

And since hostilities imitate the damages caused by an epidemic, such infection proceeded that many settlers left the area. Everything dealing with provisions was missing throughout the south, and the northern part lacked the necessary items for the sugar mills such as wood, forms, bricks, tiles, and crates. Because of this the mills had to close. With production halted, commerce ceased, which stopped the payments and increased the hunger, to the eternal harm of the public.

The governor well realized the gravity and importance of this damage, but he also saw how impossible it was to extinguish the fire of sedition with the soldiers and people of this community, since excessive levies and expenses made upon them had never had any effect. For example, in the year 1660 the governor Francisco Barreto de Meneses ordered at considerable expense to the common exchequer that a royal highway to serve for wagons be opened through the entangled forest. The field master, Pedro Gomes, then governor of the people of the land, was in charge and was given four companies of infantry with many other men and Indian slaves. Landing in the port of Cachoeira, they were to march north sixty leagues until arriving at a place called Orobó, where they would build a strong

The barbarians overrun the southern villages below and in other places

Damages caused by the barbarians

Impossibility of a remedy to quell the barbarians

Governor Francisco Barreto de Meneses in 1660 sends Field Master Pedro Gomes with soldiers, and what happens in Orobó

house capable of furnishing lodging, having left another with a great storeroom for supplies at the halfway point in the place of Piranhas. All this was done with intolerable work, for there were days when not even two armlengths could be cleared along the way, and this with extremely great expenditure of the property of the settlers. They could not acquire or catch so much as one Indian, and the project served only to make more people fall sick and die, so that it became necessary to call the task to a halt.

These and other experiences had the governor perplexed, not knowing what could be done with barbarians, who are like birds of prey that scarcely grab the quarry before they rip it up, not leaving in their retreat any sign of their trail.

Governor Alexandre de Sousa [Freire] appeals to the people of São Paulo to conquer the barbarians

Finally, it was decided to write to the senate of the town of São Paulo, offering in the name of His Highness lawful favors and awards to all those who might wish to undertake the conquest of the barbarians, for as people more versed in their language and style of warfare, [such a conquest] would be easier for the Paulistas than for the people of this town. And it was arranged according to the conditions set below.

Governor Francisco de Távora asks for help to defend Angola

But in the meantime another difficulty was added to those this town was already experiencing. The governor of Angola, Francisco de Távora, requested that men and horses be sent from here and others be advised to do the same. Angola had suffered a great defeat at the hands of the duke of Sonho, who had left it bereft of people, and if he were to attack again it would be in great danger.[11]

Miserable state of this place in the year 1671

That was the miserable condition of this place: commerce halted, the royal treasury empty, [the land] overrun with barbarians, the city of Sergipe standing firm in its rebellion, hunger running rampant, the infantry unpaid—and all of these things causing a general dismay.

But, because God punishes more as a father than as a cruel judge, He stopped our storm-tossed ship and wanted us to embark in another of good hope, which had arrived at this port after seven days of May [had passed]. It had brought us the [most memorable] thing of the century in which we live, a governor that the position was seeking, not a man who was seeking to be governor—this during the time that they offered His Highness 32,000 ducats for the public needs. His name was Afonso Furtado de Castro do Rio de Mendonça, which always for this state will be of glorious memory.

Entrance of Governor Afonso Furtado de Castro do Rio de Mendonça, May 8, 1671

He made his entrance on the eighth of May, leaving Nossa Senhora de Montserrate, where he went immediately upon setting foot on land, and took possession of the government at the Jesuit school.[12] It was a day that was widely celebrated because this place could see, as it has been said, that they were now to have a governor who had been sought to fill the position, and not one looking for a position to fill. But Heaven, which had brought him, demonstrated with repeated salvos that he belonged more to it than to the earth.

The sky was turbulent, the hills seemed to tremble at the stupendous noise of thunder and lightning

The next day he endeavored to learn from an intelligent person who were the people who gathered at the palace, regarding both their occupations and their relations. From this investigation he discovered that there were some among the most principal persons who did not speak to one another. And so he called them to him and made them friends, telling them it was not right that there be hatreds

The first day of his governorship he puts in accord all those who are to serve him and who have been [at odds]

A GOVERNOR AND HIS IMAGE

Peace for him who takes pleasure in it is the same as the manna for the people of God

and quarrels among those who were to appear in his presence. All acceded to his wishes with much pleasure, rendering him thanks. He exercised in this his first action that which Christ, Our Savior, so commended to his disciples: "That in my presence is a kind of divinity, for where it is, so is God," an effect which we learned would not be missing from the heart of our hero.

He places the services of a soldier before the supplications of the mighty to make him captain

If the above was his first action, the second was to discover the quality of the posts that were vacant, to fill them, the judicial as well as the military. Seeing that Antônio Telles, chief constable of this place, had ceded the position of captain of the infantry, he gave the post to a soldier called Luís Cardoso, who had served as adjutant for twenty years.[13] In this way and by means of good information, he provided for everything. For princes cannot know everyone.

He helps Angola with men and with horses

With the speed the situation demanded, he sent four ships to Angola with four companies and some horses, thanking the owners of the ships for participating.

He calms the tumults of Sergipe de El-Rey

In the same way, he turned his attention to quelling the rebellion of Sergipe de El-Rey, pardoning the populace, as his predecessor had already tried to do, and imprisoning the guilty, some of whom still remain in prison.[14]

He sends infantry to avoid the damages of the barbarians

With Angola succored and Sergipe at peace, he decided to send companies of infantry to the southern towns as well as to other posts, wherever the enemy was attacking. In this way he obliged the settlers not to desert their land, which would only intensify the lack of supplies.

All these aforementioned things put in order, he did everything possible to send forth the Paulistas who had recently arrived. To accomplish this he ordered the colonels to tell the captains of each district to conduct and remit all the supplies that were divided among them, sending them by land and sea to the port of Cachoeira, in care of Francisco Barbosa, who would give them a receipt for their discharge.

He orders the preparation of the conquest of the barbarians

He ordered them to make ready with all due care the supplies that were to be given to the white men as well as to the friendly Indians: tools, hatchets, sickles, firearms, powder, and bullets.

He orders that the supplies of the Paulistas and their aides be readied

At the same time, he arranged for João Peixoto Viegas, Field Master Antônio Guedes de Brito, and Captain Major Bras Rodrigues Adorno to be named to lead the friendly Indians of their areas so that, united with the Paiäiäs of the southern towns and the [Indian] settlements of the king in Cachoeira, they might march with the Paulistas.[15]

He orders all persons who have friendly Indians to send them to Cachoeira

It was commanded that everything be prepared by João de Matos de Aguiar, Knight of the Habit of Christ, a person who, because of his quality and scrupulosity, had been named by the council of this city to take charge of the treasury and the preparation of all necessary operations.[16] He ordered them to be brought before the purveyor of the treasury so that, in the arrangements with the Paulistas, complete satisfaction might be ensured. It was all done with great care, and what was agreed upon was the following:

> *Conditions by which the Paulistas went down to conquer the barbarians*

Item: That they would be granted an open campaign
Item: That the prisoners would be theirs

Item: That the leaders of the people would receive the salary that the military receives
Item: That the same would be accorded to the captains and the soldiers
Item: That in the same way they would be supplied and aided
Item: That they would be given boats and carts to carry the supplies and conduct the prisoners to their land
Item: That for this service they would submit formal documents in order to receive from His Highness all the honors due them

List of the leaders, captains and soldiers, and other men:

LEADERS

Item: Governor of the Conquest, Estevão Ribeiro Baião Parente
Item: Captain Major, Bras Rodrigues de Arzão
Item: Sergeant Major, Antônio Soares Ferreira
Item: Chaplain Major, Gaspar Luba

CAPTAINS

Item: Gaspar Velho
Item: Francisco Mendes
Item: Feliciano Cardoso
Item: Manuel Gonçalves Freitas
Item: João Viegas Xortes
Item: João Amaro Maciel Parente
Item: Vasco da Mota
Item: Manuel de Inojosa, of the friendly Indians

Item: Soldiers and Indians—314[17]

His Grace ordered and commanded the purveyor of the treasury, João de Matos de Aguiar, to satis-

LIFE OR FUNEREAL EULOGY 49

fy the Paulistas under the agreed conditions. He did this, taking care of it through the treasury of the town council of the city, of which he was treasurer, and dispatching them the first part of June in ten ships to the port of Cachoeira, where we shall leave them in order to relate the following.

The purveyor of the treasury satisfies the Paulistas and sends them off the first part of June 1671

None of the above hindered our hero in his orderly dispatch of the political government, because his doors were never closed. Nor did he deny his presence to the most humble, always observing political and religious composure in receiving ecclesiastics, prelates of the religious orders, visiting them in their convents and attending their private celebrations. If with some he was severe, it was by order of His Highness.

Honorific way in which he treats the ecclesiastical estate

From the first day of his government he elected to accompany the Blessed Sacrament every day, going to visit the sick whether it rained or whether there were great winds, despite the distance and bad roads full of mudholes or the sicknesses that he might suffer. I stated when I started this work that I was going to do no more than refresh your memory by repeating what you saw and understood, Noble Brazilians, save, I repeat again, by means of [the comparison] I am going to give. For by dint of my obligation I am forced to report the words and deeds of this our hero during his complete governorship, among them the following:

He accompanies the Blessed Sacrament every day

The eighteenth of November this year will be the 2,515th anniversary in which the prophet Jonah, passenger of a ship, was thrown from the mouth of a whale onto the powerful shores of Nineveh to announce to the Babylonian monarch his destruction. Because of that, he covered himself with ashes and ordered all his subjects to do great

On January 18 news arrives of what has happened in Odivelas

penance. When another traveler, although not a prophet, called Francisco de Lima arrived at these shores of America, he entered the palace and delivered bad news, not as Jonah to Sardanapalus with threats of future harm, nor as that which the people of God had upon seeing that the coffer of God had remained in the hands of the Philistines. No, in reality if not in shadows, it consisted of a sacrilege made to a living God, sanctified in the custody of the parish of Odivelas, near Lisbon.[18] Hearing of it caused our hero to grow weak from terror. Recovering his strength, although still showing in his mournful manner and sorrowful face his sadness, he ordered the following:

Our hero makes manifest his feelings concerning such an event

He commanded that the windows be shut and that mourning clothes be made for him and for all his household, and that in the evening there be no ordinary entertainment with gambling.

He ordered that the two senates, both the ecclesiastic and the secular, be made privy to the news so that they could do as he, which they did, preparing extensive mourning.[19]

He commanded all the army officers—such as the field masters, sergeant majors and lieutenant generals, captains, standard-bearers, and sergeants—to dress in mourning and to cover their drums and prepare the guards with banners furled and gun carriages reversed.

Having first advised the Royal Tribunal of Justice to order its ministers to follow this example, he commanded the same of the other tribunals, that of the treasury and that of the customs house; but being noble and good men they had [already] dressed in mourning without [awaiting his] orders.[20]

He commanded the same of all the municipal councils of this jurisdiction.

He ordered the purveyor of the treasury, Antônio Lopes Ulhoa, to drape the main chapel of the cathedral in mourning—the site where they were to solemnize their affliction—and to provide candles for the divine offices.

He advised the governors of the diocese to invite the prelates of the religious orders to officiate by turn at the masses in which there were to be sermons. And the senate commanded that there be three days of fasting and eight days of sermons, with all the tribunals attending, and with a general penitential procession in which all the religious orders and parishes were to take part.

Invitation to a general meeting

The aforementioned occurred January 30, the day on which the Catholic Church celebrates the memory of the final and universal judgment, and it was the greatest exhibition ever seen in Bahia: great for the motive of its being held, great for the care with which it was conducted, and great for the large number of penitents who with diverse instruments mortified their flesh. The father superior of the Sacred Company of Jesus, Inácio Faia, gave the funereal and mournful prayer.[21]

General procession on the day of universal judgment

Eight days of sermons and eight nights of many processions with unprecedented exhibitions and never-before-seen penitences followed this general demonstration. There were so many and they were of such diverse nature that they furnished copious material for Father Superior Francisco de Matos to make a learned compendium of his observations; and I, although rustic in the light of his eloquence, made another, including in it the magnificent and generous apparatus of a notable triumph to Christ crucified, such that it will please me to give some mention of it here, if the length of the paper permits me to do so.[22] To show how powerful an example our hero was with his actions, I shall say that the [demonstration] I saw in the palace of Madrid in the year 1623, for a similar situation, could not be compared to this triumph, nor could the one in Seville in the year 1635, for the case of the village of Tuxliman, eight leagues from Brussels, carried out by the soldiers of the Prince of Orange, in which they gave the Blessed Sacrament to the horses.[23]

I shall pass over in silence the great things carried out by our hero. But there will be pens of a higher sphere that will want to enjoy the glory of such an honorific occupation. Just as Mother Nature adorns her better parts, bad luck was not missing amid the good of our hero. With so many counterweights in his happinesses, it is appropriate to repeat here what a poet of Granada said of an occurrence that took place there fifty-three years [ago], which was as follows.

Fatal event during the acclamation of Philip IV, year 1622

"King Philip III died in the year 1622, and his son Philip IV inherited the crown, which was announced to the council so that he might be acclaimed king.[24] The acclamation was planned for the Feast of St. James and was celebrated by all of the governor's council, the judiciary, and artisan representatives; and the Royal Banner was accompanied by 100 gaily dressed horsemen and many kinds of drums and musical instruments.

"I found myself in the Plaza of Viva Rambla next to a platform that had been hung with rich draperies for such a function and was full of people, as will be seen in what I am going to describe.

"Scarcely had the Banner been seen in the plaza when a five-story house fell over and five of its columns killed 400 persons and changed the sumptuous treatment of worldly glories into a funereal spectacle of its greatest essence. Without touching my feet to the ground, I was carried from the plaza by the movement of the crowd, entering by Calle de los Fundidores and leaving by Sacatín, which is the main street, impelled by the initial movement of the people all the way." Those glories were converted into the sorrows that the poet saw, and he said among other couplets by which he related the story these which I am here applying to the happiness of our hero:

> But fate, enemy
> of things so perfect,
> all that majesty
> converted to dismal history.

By no other way and by no other fortune can we see in the words and deeds of this illustrious man a copy of that event. Some of these we shall relate according to the times in which they occurred, the glorious occasions and the unhappy ones, but with one reminder: that the happy ones we shall find to be the result of his judgment, and the unhappy ones to be caused by the false judgments of others, through many coalitions.

When our hero came from Portugal, it was the result of the variety of these events, which brought in one hand, in one and the same center, these two parallel lines of fortune, similar to those of Jacob and Esau, who did not entertain the same kind of fortune. From the notices that I had, its quality consisted of two functions His Highness charged

Equality is not enough for merit when there is opposition of the stars

our hero with: the first that he search for some mines of saltpeter, silver, and amethysts that were said to be near Rio Verde; the second, the conquest of the barbarians.[25] Let us leave the sheet doubled here and see the progress of the Paulistas, who left in the year 1671—and now we are in 1672, a time in which a ship at the bar requests our aid by cannon shot. We shall describe this first, before joining the Paulistas.

His Highness sends two ships to India under [command of] General João Correia de Sá

His Highness came personally to Paço de Arcos to order this ship to set sail for India with another carrying the appointed governor of India, João Correia de Sá. It left March 21 of this year. Its admiral was Jerônimo Carvalho, and it was called *São Pedro de Rates*. It had been built at a cost of 340,000 ducats, according to accounts that it is said were manifested by the Marqués de Frontera. It carried as passengers the archbishop of Goa, the Conde de Vila Pouca and his wife, and Luís Barbalho, sent as purveyor of the royal treasury of India.

Having embarked on the twenty-first of March, within three days the ship was in sight of the island of Madeira and from there took the route to the Canary Islands. There, the people began to fall ill with fevers to such an extent that it became an epidemic, and one day they had to bury eleven people at sea.

The ship, São Pedro de Rates, *arrives July 6, headed for India*

Having endured innumerable travails they finally planned to round the Cape of Good Hope, when such a storm came up that the mainmast was broken. Thus they arrived at the bar of Bahia on the sixth of July with fewer people, and of those on board almost all were sick.[26]

As soon as our hero heard of the matter, he ordered that help be given wherever necessary. When the ship landed, he commanded that the principal passengers be lodged in separate houses, sending them many refreshments, and sending to a certain person of importance one thousand gold escudos not to publicize the service. He ordered the sick to be taken to the hospital, and commanded that the well be provided for, adding them to the companies of the infantry.

Having accomplished the above, he called a meeting of the officials of the harbor, the caulkers and the men schooled in navigation, and together they went on board the ship. He ordered them to examine it carefully and attend to all its needs. After they had finished their investigation, he called them for consultation. All were in accord with respect to the need for new masts and careening, things that required much time. Thus, the monsoon for sailing to India would be lost, and His Highness should be advised so that he might indicate his pleasure. Such a resolution did not satisfy our hero for two reasons. The first was that the ship was new and should not need careening, which necessitated the most time and money. The second was the replacement of the masts, which could be accomplished only with application and hard work. On the other hand, canceling the journey would mean great harm to the treasury of His Highness and to the passengers.

Owing to this consideration, he ordered the supply master to send carpenters, with due haste, into the forests of Field Master Pedro Gomes to cut the masts and the other lumber that he so graciously offered.[27] It was done in this manner, and he came to the harbor many days, remaining there to eat,

He orders assistance for the ship

He orders lodging for the important people

He orders hospitalization for the sick and succor for the healthy

He visits the ship and consults with maritime officials, who decide it cannot sail

He resolves that the ship will set sail

The ship is prepared and he is on board when they raise the masts

He pawns his silver to Francisco da Gama to send off the ship after soliciting his friends

and within a short time the royal main hoist was constructed to carry the masts, which, so that no harm might befall, were to be put on board. That same day he gave a splendid banquet [on board] for everyone of importance who attended, and he ordered that the more than 300 men who were working the winches also be fed. And having provided everything necessary, such as 150 new infantrymen, 600 casks of drinking water, provisions, and other necessities, on the fifth of December at 3:00 in the morning they cast off with the following poem affixed to the mast.

Sonnet

    Without a mast, without sails, without rigging,
the bread molding and the people miserable,
almost submissive to your shipwreck
you arrived at this port, O Timber.
    Scarcely did you arrive when the serene
dispositions of an ardent reign
restored you completely to an excellent state
and what were your ruins are now your sirens.
    Turn, then, and enjoy the Fortune
that just before your doom you found
in this river of your glories—hope:
    The sky-blue crystal flows in fair weather
and maintains this appearance from dawn
to where the sun expires.[28]

Our hero sent an account of the expenses incurred to His Highness, and he was surprised, for repairs usually cost 100 percent more here than in Portugal. He found the expenses so reasonable that the king advised our hero that it would be convenient to fit out ships here.

This year our hero was purveyor of the Holy House of Mercy, the Misericórdia, and it it is impossible to delineate in so brief a description the generosity of his splendid largess or the kindness of his charity.[29] With charity he personally visited the sick, with largess he contributed to the purse of the shamefaced poor. Let us unfold here the the sheet that we left doubled on the progress of the Paulistas.

Year 1672

Our hero is purveyor of the Holy House of Mercy

The Paulistas had left in ten ships, and having reached the port of Cachoeira, they went to find lodging and make storage sheds near the house of Francisco Barbosa, where they waited four days for the friendly Indians. When these had come, they marched out under the command of Captain Major Bras Rodrigues Adorno toward Aporá.

When they arrived, they were lodged for fifteen days, waiting for the Governor of the Conquest. Once there, he commanded them to march back to the fort of Piranhas, thirty leagues from Aporá, through paths made rugged by the growth of brush in the thirteen years that had passed since they had been opened up by Field Master Pedro Gomes in the time of Governor Francisco Barreto.

The Paulistas march from Aporá thirty leagues to the fort of Piranhas

They remained at the strong house seven days, after which they marched a little less than another thirty leagues through the same kind of rough paths to the fort of Orobó. After they had rested, they continued four leagues in search of the Indian village called Tabaçú, which with two others they found deserted. The barbarians had left only one scout to take them news of the arrival of our people, which he would not have been able to do if he had not seen the flame of a lamp, which warned him of their arrival. The barbarian shot an arrow

They arrive at Orobó and continue on to the villages of Tabaçú

and led his people away at the time that the horses of the fiery sun bathed themselves in the fresh water just as they do in an ocean. There, then, among the horror of the shadows, necessity found paths by which the barbarians could escape the rigor of paying their due, leaving with fear and pain their poor huts burning to the sound of the repeated cries of women, old people, and children. But is it not a wonder that the shadows that opened the way of escape for the barbarians were the very things that closed it to our men, for they did not know where to advance. The night passed, and with the light they saw only the miserable ruins, and they saw no trace of where the barbarians had gone, for as it has been said, the rear guard covers up all trace of their footsteps.

At the end of three days the Governor of the people of this conquest arrived, and he was sorry that the barbarians had not been surprised. He sent several troops in search of them. But because they had such a lead, they could not be overtaken, and the troops found only seven, who were of little importance.

From this march they retreated to the first village, and from there the Governor sent some troops to Otinga, where there were friendly Indians, but they had fled just as ours had, and there were no provisions. The Paulistas had to retire to the city without having accomplished any more than to bring in seven barbarians as prisoners.

Because we are in the year 1672, in which our hero is exercising the office of purveyor of the Holy House, it is only fitting that we not forget one of his great deeds. But first we shall set down

The barbarians set fire to the villages and escape because it is night

The Paulistas retire to the city with only seven captives

the foundation on which such a great accomplishment was to be constructed, and it is as follows:

In the previous year, the time at which they were finishing the construction, the purveyor of the Holy House had been Francisco Fernandes da Ilha, knight of the Order of Santiago.[30] Moved by the honor and glory of God, he not only finished the building at his own cost, but left it a golden splendor—all of it: the chancel, the body of the church, the retable, the principal arch, the ceiling of the nave of the church with rich paintings of the life of Our Lady, lecterns, walls of tile, and a choir with a tower and a room for the sick. Wishing to crown such a notable task, he attempted to command that they prepare, as they did, a silver Tabernacle so that the sick might have the Last Sacrament, the true remedy for any accident. But even such a just petition was not strong enough for the councilmen to grant the request, and the Tabernacle had to remain in the Sacristy.

Deeds done by Francisco Fernandes da Ilha, as purveyor of the Holy House

But as time does not pass in vain, it attempted to collect from him the many years that it had spent with him, or at least not to guarantee him [more time] than was ordered by the Most High, perhaps in order to reward him with better coin than that which he had spent in His service. This great and magnanimous man recognized this, and thus he attempted to dispose of his property, which then amounted to 180,000 ducats. Of that, he left 16,000 to the Holy House so that from its interest eight poor orphan maidens might marry each year. But not even this did he accomplish, for his son-in-law, Field Master Nicolão Aranha, brought suit against it saying that such a large bequest could not be made, because he had grandchildren [to be provided for]. Thus the maidens were not able to marry. This is the foundation; let us go to the building that pertained to our hero, a deed that had its origin in the following.[31]

We are at the twenty-first of April, 1672, the day on which, at the end of a twenty-five-year period of a vacant See, the Most Reverend Father Estevão dos Santos, regular canon of [the church of] São Vicente, arrived at this port [to serve] as universal pastor of this territory.[32] Our hero paid very special court to him, and on the day of his arrival accompanied him from the church to his house. From him he received permission for the Blessed Sacrament to be in the Holy House, so he immediately ordered the silver Tabernacle that had remained in the Sacristy for so long to be placed on the high altar.

He obtains permission from the bishop to place the Blessed Sacrament in the Holy House

But our hero, being so prudent and politic, observed that it was not proper to dispose of such majesty without making use of proper ministers. Thus he arranged with the board that they provide as many as might be proper and necessary; the proposition was accepted by all, without taking into account the great expense that such a mighty effort might entail.

He deals with the board and they name ten chaplains to sing the liturgy continually

They then searched for ten chaplains, to whom they decreed a stipend of 1,000 reales each year, and 2,500 to the head chaplain and 1,500 to the master of the chapel, adding two acolytes to be paid to serve the choir and the altar, all to assist during the canonical hours.

Having taken care of the above-mentioned details, he thought it proper to settle the dispute of the 16,000 ducats that Francisco Fernandes da Ilha had left designated for the marriage of eight orphan girls each year, in order that it be settled that the board [of the Misericórdia] pardon his daughter, Dona Francisca, from the interest. She in turn would cede the right she had, for she was not to obtain what she claimed, out of respect for the mediator.³³

He reconciles the dispute of the 16,000 ducats left so that eight orphans might marry each year

Having reconciled all these things, he arranged a most solemn feast for the day on which they were to display the Blessed Sacrament, a feast in which there was to be much music and a sermon. And with this, our hero ended his year, although not his memory, as purveyor. See what a blessed year it was, and what a felicitous structure was built upon such a beautiful foundation.

He decrees a celebration with majestic pomp for the arrival of the Blessed Sacrament at the Holy House

Such an honorific deed had no sooner been accomplished when Our Lord took unto Himself the bishop, who had not exercised the office more than two months and fifteen days, and it appeared that he had come only for the great occasion.

The bishop dies the sixth of July, 1672

We are at the end of the year, when the effects of the second and unhappy line having to do with the discovery of the mines began. Who would have thought that these not being of saltpeter but of silver would have caused unhappiness?

It should be known that His Highness, may God keep him, was informed by the captain major of Sergipe de El-Rey that there were mines of saltpeter, amethysts, and silver on the Rio Verde in the mountains of Piguraça, and thus it was learned that he commissioned our hero to make all possible investigations into the case. He did so, using men who had knowledge of the territory and were wise in the ways of the land, such as Bento Suriel, a Frenchman, who for this reason was sent for and came to spend much time in the palace.[34] Afterward he sent him, accompanied by Manuel da Silva Freitas, to search for the mines.

The amethyst mines do not have effect

They went and brought back the saltpeter, and weighing their expenses against the gains made, it was found that it would not pay to continue the operation. As for the amethyst [mines], or others that might be of silver, nothing was found. And that was the first affair of the mines. Now let us see how our hero reacted to the retreat of the Paulistas and what he did about it, seeing that they did not bring back more than seven Indians although their foray had cost 20,000 ducats.

Difficulties arise so that the conquest of the barbarians cannot be continued

Notable was the sentiment of our hero, seeing the little fruit that the inhabitants had harvested from all that had been spent in an affair in which His Highness and they had shown such interest, all of which perplexed him for not just one but many reasons. First, the republic found itself exhausted without hope of finding remedy in the hands of the Paulistas. Second and more decisive, [the republic was] incapable of accepting new contributions for engagements that did not promise improvement. On the other hand, he realized that although His Highness had ordered him to effect the conquest with the funds of the Royal Treasury, they had been diminished, and this had to be considered since it was necessary to justify any determination that might have to be resolved, not only to satisfy His Highness but also the Royal Treasury.

And so, having attended to various and sundry obligations, he decided to order that a Treasury Board be formed, which is like a council, and that it should be not only ministers of this branch but a general junta of all courts, judicial and political, heads of the militia, and principal persons, in order to confer what would be most convenient to the service of the prince and the public welfare. Once they had all assembled, he spoke to them in this manner:

"It is notorious to us, gentlemen, to all of those here present, the great and public damage that the barbarians of this republic have caused. It is also notorious that my predecessors undertook many enterprises to remedy this, with great expense to the public welfare, and in particular my predecessor Francisco Barreto, who during his term ordered that the forts of Piranhas and Orobó be built without taking into account and preparing for the great expense of such an enterprise. We are undergoing the same in the undertaking ordered by Senhor Alexandre de Sousa, using new means which are the people of São Paulo, experienced and well versed in similar conquests. This being so, it falls upon me to say that although the evils continue to afflict the human body, it is the duty of the physician to continually prescribe remedies, despite the fact that some might not help. The evils that this republic is suffering are so great that there is no part that does not suffer the effects, and all parts united form a universal compendium of them. Attending to this, each part should suggest what appears best to him [the physician], for the remedy is the concern of all present as interested parties."

Speech that our hero makes to the general assembly

All had been attentive to the reasonings of our hero, but no one as much as the head of the political government of the republic,[35] as the most interested, and thus taking the floor, he said:

"We thank Your Lordship for the zeal and the love with which you treat and procure our remedy,

Response of the political governor and the interested [parties]

and we acknowledge how just is all that Your Lordship has proposed and how it behooves us to make use of the remedies so prudently proposed by Your Lordship, for necessity thus demands it.

"But, Sir, as all this is well known, so too are, Your Lordship, the many obligations with which the city finds itself today, such as 60,000 ducats to sustain the infantry, 40,000 for the dowry of Her Most Serene Highness the Queen of Great Britain, and the peace of Holland, which is always in arrears.[36] And Your Lordship knows also how much effort was expended to gather the 20,000 that were spent in this undertaking of the Paulistas, to which we must add the paucity of the fruits of their labor, and the extenuation under which, because of these reasons, the inhabitants now find themselves forced to submit anew to such an undertaking in view of the poor return to our contribution." And he had no more to say on the subject. All the citizens were of the same opinion, but they did not want to discuss it endlessly, for they were not in a state of mind to concede it. The ministers of justice and the militia insisted that the conquest be continued, for they, although with little success, were the ministers of the enterprise. But as they did not have the wherewithal to manage the undertakings, they coldly discussed the matter, and, taking the floor, our hero spoke and resolved the following:

New speech of our hero, resolving that the conquest of the barbarians be continued

"I thought, gentlemen, when I proposed this junta, that I would obtain what I desired upon proposing it, and that was to serve God, [and] His Highness. I wish to make public that I find this has been rendered difficult, perhaps because of not having weighed the matter to the degree of its [proper] estimation.

"Well might I agree with what has been proposed here, if we were to make this conquest for [mere] fame. But we are in a more difficult position, which is to have to act by necessity. This cannot be subjected to any law, but must be done as the arm of the human body which on seeing a blow fall upon its head, attacks with the edge of the sword.

"This barbarian does not aim his blows at any parts of this republic but those which happen to be the parts that administer our sustenance and commerce, the former in the south, the latter in the north with its produce of the sugar mills. It is a necessity that must be attended to even if it be with the last breath.

"There has been no lack of those who have advised me that I could send the infantry to the estates where the barbarians appear, and that they might eat there, as here, their salary. That would be well if experience had not demonstrated that the barbarians come to seek out the captains at these estates and kill them.

"It is not a war of large [and] concerted battles, but of disconcerted and intemperate assaults. The inconveniences proposed here ask for no more than to take leave of the Paulistas, and will serve no other purpose than to give new wings to the barbarians in their acts of injustice, for they will see that neither through our [own] forces nor through those of others that we added were we able to subject them.

"And so I am of the same opinion as the physicians who, when they find the humors unbalanced in the body, purge it. The humors of the barbarians, which are the sickness of the body of this republic, are approaching imbalance because of the Paulistas.

Now that this is so, we ought to purge them by continuing the conquest—not only because it is to our advantage, but also because it is the will of His Highness to conserve his vassals; and I, in his name, heeding the lack of funds that it seems you are suffering and regardless of finding his [funds] diminished, take it upon myself to pursue the conquest at all costs, because it is the pleasure of him who sent me here to do the task. Let the fragments that remain of the funds collected from the people and under the jurisdiction of the treasurer, João Matos de Aguiar, be delivered to the royal ministers, the treasurer, and the receiver of customs duties."[37]

With great applause the resolution of our hero was heard, for which he was thanked and by which the assembly was ended.

The purveyor of the treasury is ordered to supply the Paulistas according to the contract

The next day he commanded the purveyor of the treasury to send to the expedition of the Paulistas all that they had listed as necessary.

The order is given to the colonels to send supplies

He also commanded that orders be sent to the colonels that they in turn command the captains of their districts to bring the supplies needed to the house of Francisco Barbosa at the port of Cachoeira.

Captain Major Bras Rodrigues Adorno and others in command of the friendly Indians were ordered to conduct them to the same port to be united with the Paulistas, whom they were to help. Thus it was done, at a cost of 7,244,524 *réis*.

The Paulistas quarrel among themselves; notice [of same] is received by our hero

These people had scarcely landed when the leaders quarreled among themselves—the sergeant major, the captain major, and the chaplain—against the Governor over their desire to return by land to São Paulo, and for that reason the friendly Indians deserted, not without the suspicion that they had been encouraged to do so. And so the entire affair was in such a state that not only the diligence of our hero but also the 50,000 ducats that had been spent on the two forays appeared to have been absolutely in vain.

The Governor of the Conquest reported this disorder to our Lordship by way of the adjutant, Manuel de Inojosa. When His Lordship recognized the miserable state of the affair and that if it were not remedied immediately the important business would be greatly endangered, without consulting anyone or asking for advice he ordered a ship. And without considering his own poor health he boarded, taking with him the secretary, Bernardo Vieira,[38] Lieutenant General Sebastião [de] Araújo, Sergeant Major Bento Rebelo, and the people in his service, leaving behind orders for all the colonels to follow him, and commanding that the supplies be divided as previously agreed.

Our hero sails to reconcile the Paulistas

As soon as he arrived, learning that the friendly Indians were not there, he ordered Captain Major Bras Rodrigues Adorno and Captain Francisco Pires to go and look for them and not to appear before him without them. Thus the Tupís of *Lingua geral*[39] as well as the Paiäiás and Sapoiás all came back within three days. He named as their captain Adjutant Manuel de Inojosa.[40]

He arrives at Cachoeira, makes the friendly Indians reappear, and names Adjutant Manuel de Inojosa captain

In the interim, while this was taking place, our hero did not fail to investigate the cause and motives of the mutiny and of the division, and not because the mutiny attained what it set out to do; [as it] was a thing that required severe action he thought [it necessary] to take it. In such an urgent

68 A GOVERNOR AND HIS IMAGE

situation, feigning to ignore what had happened, he called them before him, and when they had come, he said:

Speech that he makes to the leaders of the Paulistas

"You well know the great efforts that the city and now His Highness have made in order that by them what has been hoped for might be obtained, and that is the reason all are gathered here. Up to the present nothing has been accomplished, nothing. Try to work in a manner that will satisfy your obligation, for now in the present state only this is what can preserve it and this will be obtained only if love and good will unite you."

All offered to do this for him.

Favors done for the transporters of the food supplies

Having said this, there were no persons among those commissioned with the transport of arms or supplies and other things whom he did not personally instruct in their obligation, supplying them with all they needed.

He gives favors to the friendly Indians

He did the same with the friendly Indians, ordering that they be paid and giving them tools and other things so that they might be content.

Splendid table for the colonels and important leaders and more than 300 people

He invited all the important personages assisting him, colonels, field masters, captains, and noblemen, of whom there were more than thirty, to eat with him the entire fifteen days that he was there, sustaining more than 300 people of greater and and lesser rank.

Field Master Antônio Guedes de Brito helps with seventy Indians for the foray

Not missing this campaign was Field Master Antônio Guedes de Brito, who brought at his own cost from Jacobina with the white people, a company of seventy friendly Indians from his ranches.

In the following manner, that is to say, in the aforementioned manner, our hero dispatched the troops, and although the discomfort of the housing and his poor health demanded that he return home to rest, he did not wish to do so until he had dispatched a second shipment of provisions. Having sent this forth, he went to receive the fleet, which was entering the port. Let us leave him who gloriously accomplished so great a task that throughout the coming centuries his name is to become immortal.

Our hero sails and comes to receive the fleet that was arriving

And now that we have demonstrated, although in limited lines, what was not possible to explain in many, let us leave, as has been said, our hero and look again at the course taken by the Paulistas.

When they departed, let it be known that they left Captain Manuel da Costa at the house of Francisco Barbosa to receive and remit the provisions (which did not cost less than five *patacas* each *alqueire*) that were being sent there. This he did with great care.

The Paulistas followed the same path that they had followed in the previous journey to Piranhas and Orobó, searching for signs of it, which seemed to serve as a guide to them to reach the end of that vast region.

From this place of Orobó they marched fifty leagues toward the south, and although they took with them experienced men, those Indians who had been captured during the previous journey, there were no paths by which to advance except those they cut open with a billhook over the very rocky crags. There was a remarkable lack of water except for that which they could squeeze from the roots of the *palo blando*; for asperity, as chosen by the barbarians, served as their defense.[41]

These people had lived with the harshness and mystery of these deserts for two months when on the second of July they caught sight of two scouts who, immediately upon seeing our people, went to warn theirs. We followed them for three days, never drinking more water than that of some *carabatas*, which is that dew they retain in their large leaves.[42]

The Paulistas march 120 leagues to arrive at the village of Otinga and find the Indians have retreated

In this manner they arrived at a small village called Otinga after nightfall.[43] But all the barbarians had already departed, leaving [only] a troop of bowmen to divert our people. After shooting their arrows, those barbarians went to join the rest. And when dawn broke there was no one there, which obliged our forces to retreat one league.

The barbarians contact the Paulistas in the guise of peace

At nine o'clock in the morning some troops of the barbarians came upon a peace mission, which Captain Manuel de Lemos advanced to meet, and in a peaceful manner he told them in their own tongue of *Topin* [Tupí?] that they [the Paulistas] were not Brazilians but a different people, their relatives who would be able to eat with them, to marry their daughters to their sons, and their sons to their daughters. The Indians demonstrated a willingness to accept what he said, but falsely, for they had come only to examine us—because, upon retiring, four men shot arrows at us.

The next day our people went into the deserted village, and the barbarians attacked them. Declaring a truce, they requested three days to deliberate their surrender, which was granted them. But they, more astute than we, took advantage of the three days to withdraw more of their people, and retreating at the end of the period they shot at one man.

Our people fortified themselves at this site to await the arrival of the Governor of the Conquest, who, immediately upon arriving, ordered that the barbarians be followed to see which way they had gone. In pursuit they captured three Indians, among them the son of one of their leaders who would be the equivalent to our governor. They imprisoned him and sent the other two to persuade the Indians to submit. This was done, because it would be impossible to defeat them any other way.

Seeing that they did not return, the Paulistas marched on for thirty leagues through dense undergrowth, with no water but that of some plants whose roots were like onions, which, upon squeezing them, furnished some moisture. When there were no plants the people drank their own urine. At the end of the thirty leagues, they were following the São Francisco River, and the barbarians, feeling confident that not even birds could pass over such a sterile land, were so dispersed and careless that it was easy to overcome them. The leader, the father of him whom we have already mentioned as having been imprisoned, helped greatly by delivering not only his own village but two others. These villages were called in the twisted tongue Jacuasui, Joiaicà Capitua Topins, and Otinga, and their leader Sacambuaçu, which in our language means "big fish."

The Paulistas march thirty leagues, following the barbarians until they catch them

It would be well to note here the manner in which the Paulistas conquer the barbarians, the way I have come to understand it.

Way in which the Paulistas conquer the barbarians

When these Paulistas forage out to conquer barbarians, they make one of their members the head and give him the title of Governor of Arms. He decides where his camp will be, sends his troops, which they call *bandeiras*, of white men with firearms and friendly Indians with bows and arrows.

As soon as any of the bandeiras encounter these barbarians, they feign that their leader is near with

Entrance of the Paulistas and friendly Indians in the plaza of the palace, August 1672

many troops and that surrender is necessary, for otherwise they would be killed with firearms— making them understand what this means by then shooting at animals, which they kill, something that frightens the barbarians greatly. If they act rebellious, the Paulistas lead them to understand that they will be pursued even if they scatter throughout the land, and this is why the Paulistas have reached even as far as the Spanish Indies.[44] By these means or similar ones they subdued them, allowing them to remain armed with bows and arrows with no distrust or fear that they might rebel, which for such a barbarous people, is saying a great deal.

Well, when the three villages were defeated by the Paulistas, despite the many people, not more than 600 souls were found cataloged in this city who, disembarking at the wharf of the Jesuit fathers, marched up to the gates of the city, at the Carmelite convent, and from there made their entry to the palace.[45]

This was during the last days of the month of August, a happy and festive time for all the populace, for at last they saw beneath their yoke those who had caused them so much suffering. They came, or made their entrance, marching as they were accustomed, which was as follows: the procession consisted of the Governor of the Conquest, the vanguard with the white people of the troop with firearms, wearing on their heads helmets plumed with feathers of parrots and macaws, his [the governor's] page on horseback with the shield and bearing the staff of command, and the rest of the leaders and captains following with their men in the position that pertained to each. Between companies marched, as I have said, according to custom, the friendly Indians, the men armed with the weapons that they use, bows and quivers full of arrows. The young men were like Adam, some with their bodies painted blue, others covered with white feathers; being a gala occasion, the lower lips were pierced and plugged with white plates of bone, and they came playing some military instruments in their fashion.

The fashion in which they march, their manner and dress

As for the women, only some flounces made of grasses covered their feminine parts, and on their heads and backs they bore the trappings of their huts and families: the net in which they slept and, in a basket that they called a *panacu*, the things of their kitchens.[46] In their arms and at their breasts were their babes, and on their backs [with] their [little] hands clasped in front, those who could not walk, and the bigger children holding hands one with another—the women appearing like any [mother] hen who with her wings protects and covers all her chicks. Many of the women had their faces painted blue, and as some were not ugly, they appeared to be wearing horrible masks.

Manner of the women

These people marched alone, man or woman, one behind the other, playing at intervals their instruments, which, if to us seemed barbarous but happy, to them were sad.

And thus they entered the plaza, the Governor of the Conquest bringing as a trophy the principal leader of the Indians, whom we have mentioned before. Our hero descended to the door of the palace to welcome and embrace him [the governor], but the principal leader of the Indians, noting that he was not treated in the same manner, threw himself in our hero's arms, saying in his native tongue, "Embrace me, for in my land I am also the governor as you are in yours." Our hero graciously accepted the confidence and satisfied him, commanding that they be provided lodging near the church of Vitoria, outside the city walls, where he sent them many refreshments. This being, then, the second part of the happy line, let us see what happens with the second part of the unhappy line.

The captain major of Sergipe de El-Rey, João Vieira, comes by order of His Highness so that he can be given what he might request for exploration of the mines

We have said that the captain major of Sergipe de El-Rey was the one who informed His Highness that there were mines in this state, and this captain's name was João Vieira. Now we must say that he came to this city by order of His Highness so that our hero could give him what he might seek, without inquiring why he requested it. His Lordship did so, and he went to the mountains of Itabaiana, eighty leagues from this city. It is said that he had extracted some stones from there and had taken them to Pernambuco, where he sailed with them to Portugal. While he was there it was learned that they were assayed, and he told no one until an important person from Castile, named Don Rodrigo de Castelo Branco, arrived, of whom it was learned that he had been reared in the management of the mines of Spain.[47] Notice of his ability was given to His Highness, who ordered that he take charge of the assaying of those stones. And in doing so, he demonstrated that his knowledge was a thing useful to the royal crown. In virtue of this he was given honors and made a petty nobleman of his house, as well as the general administrator of all the mines of this state, with 60,000 *maravedís* per month if there were mines, or 30,000 if there were none, plus personal income.[48] With all these honors he arrived here at the end of the year 1673, where we shall leave him curing some ailments, in order to re-

Honors that His Highness confers upon Don Rodrigo de Castelo Branco so that he might come to discover the mines

late what had been happening to our hero during this time.

In this year 1673 our hero remembered that the hermitage that he had visited when he had arrived from Lisbon, that of Nossa Senhora de Montserrate, was in bad repair; and he asked his lieutenant general, Sebastião de Araújo, if he would not like to take charge of ordering stonecutters and carpenters to do all repairs that might be necessary so that all might be reconstructed. And so it was done at once.

He orders the rebuilding of the hermitage of Nossa Senhora de Montserrate, 1673

As soon as he saw it completed, he asked the secretary, Bernardo Vieira Ravasco, to take charge of making plans for a great feast to celebrate the rebuilding of Nossa Senhora de Montserrate with the same perfection that he used for the celebrations of the great and honorific deeds of governors.[49]

He asks the secretary of state to plan a great celebration for Nossa Senhora

It seems that never in his life had this gentleman heard a voice so resonant and so melodious as his [Afonso Furtado's], for he is never so accomplished as when he exercises similar functions. It was as if the temple were that of Solomon and the treasury that of the royal prophet David. He arranged the hangings in such a way that he united with the smallness of that building all that art and culture were accustomed to deduce from nature. And I, in what I say, can do no more than follow the steps of a poor painter who, upon being ordered to portray a giant on a limited canvas, depicts on it the smallest portion of his hand so that from it the greatness of the figure might be understood.

Excellence of the decoration of the church

The mass was celebrated with sonorous music, and the eulogies with the great attention that the extreme eloquence of the distinguished priests

Divine and human entertainment

knew how to consign to that source of so much light, the Most Holy Mary.

Plays are staged at sea

This had to do with the divine celebration, and in what pertained to the human, not even the waters of Neptune were missing in the midst of artful secular ceremonies and discreet plays, nor songs of innocent sirens, which delight with their conceits the ears and the souls of the public. This and other pious but extravagant expenses did not hinder our hero from accepting the post of minister of the Third Order of Saint Francis, which he administered with two charges—a personal one for the obligations of the office, a spiritual one for charity.[50] Let us stop here and return to Don Rodrigo, who is now rising from his sickbed and wishes to set off for the mines.

Our hero accepts the post of minister of the Third Order of Saint Francis

Don Rodrigo leaves for the mountains of Itabaiana in search of the mines but does not find them

Having improved, Don Rodrigo sought the things he needed for his departure, such as money, tools and other things, and orders so that the jurisdictions or captaincies through which he might pass on his journey would fulfill all his needs. All was given to him, and so he left for the mountains of Itabaiana to investigate his mines.

He spent one year looking for such mines from day to day, and all he found, he had assayed; and he sent news to His Highness that from what he could understand nothing he found was of value. And so the credit they had given in Lisbon to Captain Major João Vieira, the assays of Don Rodrigo, and the expenses suffered here were all in vain. And this was the second course of events with the mines pertaining to the unhappy line. Let us see what is occurring in the happy one.

During the first days of May 1673 the Paulistas made their third expedition against the Maracás, penetrating even farther than [that area] from whence they had brought back the others—and I must excuse myself from repeating in detail here the march of these people, their intolerable travails, lack of water, and other great difficulties. Suffice to say that although their previous journey had taken four months to find the others, this journey cost even more, so in comparison with that conflict, the travails of this one must be considered. Many more than 200 leagues they labored to pass through the roughness of those uninhabitable mountains and deserts to discover them, because [the Indians] are of the sort that in order to find them it is necessary as in a rabbit hunt to release a ferret through one or another thicket, through one or another crevice. And so the troops wandered through many, many areas, making diverse circles from north to south.

Added to these tasks was the great cost of people bearing [things] on their shoulders, as the people and the horses of the convoys did. This second journey to the Maracás was made on the advice of the Indians captured in the previous journey, who had said that beyond them lived some people who had formerly come down with them to pilfer and had retreated owing to quarrels among them over the distribution of the booty.

Consider now the undertaking, the immensity of perseverance with which this people labored to oppose those whom nature itself defended. By means of these arduous tasks, one day they arrived at a lagoon that was by a lake where the Indians came down to amuse themselves and to celebrate their festivals. Realizing their presence, our people rose at the sound of shots and drums, and being unpre-

The Paulistas arrive at the Maracás and capture 1,074 persons after traveling 200 leagues

pared it was easy to overcome them, demonstrating by this object lesson that the Topis, a tribe that exceeded all others in animosity, had surrendered. They found themselves in three villages among many people, of whom only 1,074 arrived at this city. The journey cost 6,432,134 maravedís, this [surrender] having justified the cost of the convoy.

These people entered the city at the end of September, and as they were so many, the festivities with their entrance were all the greater. They were accommodated in everything they asked with regard to the march and the sums mentioned, as well as other requests. [The Indians] were provided lodging at the campgrounds until there were sailings for São Vicente, when the Paulistas sent them to their territory.[51]

The Paulistas make a fourth expedition into the [land of the] Maracás in December 1673, which takes them almost a year

At the end of December of this year 1673 our hero commanded the Governor of the Conquest to make a fourth expedition with the people he had, made up of fourteen vessels, to search the same areas for other villages that were said to be in the same [land of the] Maracás, although in much more distant locations.

Punishment is not what happens but what exists

They set off, and following the rugged and broken terrain, they suffered greater travail and discomforts in this journey, though it took them a little less than one year to finish it. To repeat here all that was told me of the sufferings, the rough terrain, the lack of water, would be endless; and I came to believe that it would have been better for these men to fight these barbarians face to face on a field of battle, leaving the end result to the hands of Fortune herself, than to suffer without danger of battle so much hunger and more thirst.

Penetrating the deserts twelve times, Captain

Manuel de Inojosa approached the [village] of the Cochos,[52] where he discovered a river 200 fathoms in breadth and apparently navigable, which the Indians called Quitose.[53] In the end no more than 400 Indians were found. They came back with these to say that the others must have fled into the interior, fearful of losing the pearl of all nature, which is liberty.

Captain Manuel de Inojosa discovers a river called Quitose

Until now, as the report that I am making indicates, there have been four campaigns by the Paulistas made at the command of our hero, all forming part of the felicitous line. But since he is under the influence of two equally strong, although diverse, fortunes, let us see what their effects are.

We are at the thirtieth of June, a time at which a ship sailing for India called *Nossa Senhora do Rosario e São Caetano* arrived. Its captain was Simão de Sousa de Távora, and it had set out at the command of Governor Alexandre de Sousa Freire, but it had been so poorly constructed by the shipping masters in Lisbon that it was unmanageable, so much so that the rudder was inoperative, and the sailors refused to continue in it.

June 30 the ship Nossa Senhora do Rosario e São Caetano arrives, captained by Simão de Sousa de Távora, headed for India, 1674

Our hero was advised of the situation, and he ordered the carpenters of the shipyard, the caulkers, and the men experienced in sailing to come to visit the ship, examine it, [and] confer with the men on board to discover what could be done to remedy the situation.

And so it was done, and the masters discovered that, according to the plan, the geometrical measurements of the masts and the rudder were not in agreement. Thus they said that the ship should undergo repairs, making the necessary changes and enlarging the rear portion to reshape the rudder.

80 A GOVERNOR AND HIS IMAGE

The sailors try to spend the winter [here], not continuing to India because of the ship's defects

Our hero succeeds in repairing the ship so that it is seaworthy

The royal ministers of São Vicente advise that mines exist in Paranaguá

The people of the ship opposed this advice, saying that besides being a great undertaking, there was no certainty that such repairs would remedy the situation, and that His Highness should be advised and in the interim all should await his resolution.

Our hero was not in agreement with this opinion, and he commanded that work be started, assuring the more indolent of the ship that if it did not meet with their approval, they could stay on land and he would put others in their place. All this was done by our hero as a man who weighed the inconveniences that similar delays bring about and how noxious they are to the Royal Treasury.

When what the masters had ordered had been executed, and the masts and rudder had been set into place, and they had been provided with all their needs, he commanded them to make a trial run. They admitted that all the previous faults had been remedied by the repairs they had opposed, and those who were in the service of their prince could not do otherwise. And on the seventeenth of November the ship sailed out of the harbor, and now we must return to that other line this ship crossed, and thus we shall go back and look for it.

It is known that [besides] the two events that had taken place in the mines—the one by Bento Suriel in the mountains of Piguraça next to Rio Verde, the second by Don Rodrigo in the mountains of Itabaiana, both with little success—there were others in the mountains of Paranaguá, some 400 leagues distant from this city, which had been made known by the captain major of São Vicente, Francisco de Figueredo, and Sergeant Major Sebastião Velho de Lima, Purveyor of the Royal Treasury. Claims are not bad if the judgment that corresponds to them is able to evaluate them. [Those claims] were no less than to say that His Highness would receive greater returns from the mines than those received by the king of Spain from the mountain of Potosí.⁵⁴

This same news that they gave to our hero was sent to His Highness, who, in addition to the general orders that he sent to him to name ministers, wrote to Don Rodrigo to advise what would be necessary to send to São Vicente, and having done so he should go see João Peixoto Viegas, from whom he had news that there existed mountains in his territory that had proven to contain silver.

With these orders and with the advice of Don Rodrigo, our hero sent a small vessel with orders to go via Rio de Janeiro and receive on board Frei João de Graniça of the Order of Saint Francis—a man who knew much about mines, to whom he was writing that he should join the officials of São Vicente, and that he should judiciously verify through assays that he might make of the rocks taken from the mountain of Paranaguá the value they might render. They complied and set off. He advised the ministers of São Vicente the same, naming them in virtue of the general orders received from His Highness to administer the aforementioned operation.

As soon as the priest had arrived at São Vicente and met with the captain major and the others, they called the justice and scribe and together went to the indicated mountain. Removing rocks, they made three assays from which they drew out of every ten pounds of rock one small bar that contained the value of a Spanish *real de ocho*. This I can swear to from documents that I saw. On this

1674

News is sent to His Highness and he orders what is to be done

Our hero orders them to go via Rio de Janeiro so that Frei João de Graniça can go to make the assays

Essence of the assays of the mines of Paranaguá

Offers that the ministers of São Vicente make to His Highness

occasion they sent a rock from a gold mine, which would not be too bad if it were known from which mountain it was taken. It weighed ten ounces and rendered one and one-half *adarmes*.

With these first fruits the men wrote to His Lordship that the output of the mines promised to be greater than that of the mountain of Potosí, which we mentioned—and I saw this information in letters that they wrote to important ministers. They were given permission to send bars with new notices, instead of the stones that were sent to be assayed by Don Rodrigo [earlier], which made it important that it be kept secret. They asked His Lordship to send them an engineer to fortify the positions. They asked more: that they be sent gunpowder, shot, and tools—picks, levers, and pumps, or shovels with long handles—and all this with great enthusiasm.

Arriving at this point and censuring myself for this error and indiscreet facility, I recall something that happened to me upon entering Seville fifty-one years and twenty-eight days ago, which would make it the fifth of April in the year 1625. There were thirty-six ministers, one juror, and one artisan representative [standing] at the eighteen gates the city had. At each gate that I tried to enter I was detained in what they call the *arenal* until I would talk to those ministers. I did so, and I was asked who I was, where I had come from, and why I had come. I satisfied them, and they permitted me to enter. I wished to know the cause of such exact scrutiny and was told that letters had been written from Italy warning that some men had journeyed to Spain with the intention of infecting the waters of the rivers and wells with some powders that they were carrying, in order to kill the people. The city fathers of such a celebrated city were in such a state that they believed this fabulous tale and devised a fitting demonstration; with the river and the wells from which they drank being outside the city, they defended the city. Now let us continue. So be it.

When our hero had seen the letters, it seemed to him that here was a matter of such great importance confirmed by well-experienced men that there could be no doubt, and giving it his complete confidence, he determined that the one to carry such good news to His Highness should be his own son. And thus he sent him off with the samples, letters, and notices of all that was requested on the fifth of August of this year. Be that as it may, in this line was the vice of misfortune, and it mattered little that the provisional news he carried was happy —he could not avoid a shipwreck. And I might have to advise of worse misfortunes.

On August 5 the son of our hero leaves with the news of the mines, 1674

At the end of December of this year a ship arrived from Lisbon, and since it reported no news of his son's arrival and reported only that there had been many Moors on the coast, our hero became concerned. To relieve that worry he decided to pay a visit to Our Lady, who always relieves afflictions, and so he went to Montserrate. He had scarcely arrived at the church when a ship from the city of Oporto, in the kingdom, docked. It brought a letter from the pilot, who had given passage to the field master, who sent it from Lisbon to his wife, and she in turn sent it here to her son, Manuel dos Reis, who in turn brought it to our hero. In substance the letter said the following.

Our hero is troubled at having no news of his son

"Having arrived with prosperous fortune at the

News of the shipwreck of the field master

latitude of 38 degrees, as we were looking for land, we caught sight of two ships of Turks who, seeing us alone and unprotected in our small ship, hoisted sail to catch us.[55] And they would have done so had our ship not been so swift. Two days they pursued us, and on the last night, close to land without knowing it, the ship ran aground shortly before daybreak while the sea was more savage than choppy. The people threw themselves into the sea, thinking to save themselves on land, but the undertow of the waves submerged them so that of fifty people only eleven escaped, among whom Field Master João Furtado was miraculously included. In brief, I looked for him where they had lodged him, and [after] sending the news to Lisbon his brother, Jorge Furtado, [came] to take him away. It was fortunate that they took him to His Highness, who was as happy that he had escaped injury as he was sorry for the trouble and the risk to which he had been exposed. He [Jorge Furtado] took me to his house, where I am recuperating."[56]

Our hero gives thanks to Our Lady for the good fortune of his son

With much tenderness and sentiment, although he did not show his feelings, the brave gentleman heard the news; and seeing that his son was alive and that it was due to a mantle of Our Lady, which he had given him at the time of his departure, he withdrew and took leave of all and went to give thanks to Her who had done him such a favor. And so he returned to the city in a better state of mind than when he left.

Supplies requested are sent to the mines

As soon as he had arrived, he learned by another letter that some letters pertaining to the mines of Paranaguá had been saved, and considering what had been requested, he took care of sending an engineer as well as granting the other requests. Also,

20,000 ducats of those which had arrived in the fleet of João Rodrigues de Siqueira were sent, so that the ministers of the general company might be paid from our treasury.[57]

We have already said that His Highness sent our hero general orders to name ministers to take charge of the assays and the administration of the mines, in virtue of which he named the people mentioned. Also we said that he commanded Don Rodrigo to set off for the mountains of João Peixoto Viegas. I shall tell you what happened with the one and with the other.

Five days after His Highness issued orders to our hero empowering him to name ministers, others were given in favor of the purveyor of the treasury of Rio de Janeiro. Having received these he went to São Vicente and arrested the one named by our hero, saying that it was his authority according to orders from His Highness. And he did so many things that all was ruined. The prince is unhappy when he does not have faithful ministers. This is what was meant when someone said that it was preferable to have a bad king with good ministers than a good king with bad ministers. And in the end there were those who said that this might have been the cause of what we shall now see.

Contrary orders are given for the administration of the mines of Paranaguá and they are undone

Regarding the order of Don Rodrigo to set off for the mountains of João Peixoto, he went, and in all of his analyses he did not find silver or anything of value.

Don Rodrigo examines the mountains of João Peixoto and finds no silver

We are in the year 1675, and the fleet had arrived with the supplies for the mines and the engineer, whom our hero had sent with Sergeant Major Antônio Soares Ferreira to the town of São Vicente with the new title of adminstrator, to pre-

In November 1674 our hero sends a new administrator to the mines, with the engineer

vent the one from Rio de Janeiro from taking office. He was to make new assays to confirm the news that our hero's son had taken to Portugal, in view of the fact that there had been no further news since that time. And they left from here in November of 1674 in a good ship going and coming, for the fleet was to carry the resolution of everything.

As soon as the above-mentioned was dispatched, out hero concerned himself with the fleet that had wintered here, expecting each hour that the resolution of the mines would be forthcoming, and in addition to this ship there was another vessel to consider. But it was now almost laded by the month of January, and the news had not arrived, and seven months had passed since the samples of Pactá had come. Finally the ship was laded but it waited until February 24 when, because nothing had appeared, it sailed.

There was no respite for our hero; scarcely had he sent the fleet when he took notice of new dispatches, which brought to mind how advantageous it would be to explore a river that Captain Manuel de Inojosa had seen when he went against the Maracás. For if it were navigable from the north, from whence it flowed to the south, it would be easy to protect Bahia from the barbarians.

And so he called for the captain and charged him with the exploration of the said river, offering him not only his favors and honors but also the opportunity to act as patron on behalf of his prince. This captain was a well-qualified and well-born young man whose father had taken part in the war of Pernambuco, for which service his father was given the rank of lieutenant general, and he was obli-

The fleet leaves the twenty-fourth of February and carries no news of the mines

1675 A.D.

Our hero deals with the discovery of the Quitose River

gated to His Lordship for having made him a captain. He kissed his hand for such a great favor, offering not to return without bringing him complete news of what he desired.[58]

Then our hero gave him the necessary orders, and the purveyor of the treasury provided him and his people with all that was needed. When it was finished he set off with the people of his company and his household, taking with him Antônio Rodrigues Botão, scribe of the camp, so that he could give a faithful account of all he might see happen. And on the tenth of March he left for Cachoeira, where we shall let him go to report what was happening in the meantime.

On March 10, 1675, Captain Manuel de Inojosa leaves to explore the Quitose River

On April 15 a small ship from India arrived flying the flag of the vice-admiral, which was called *Nossa Senhora da Boa Memoria*, and on May 22 its flagship, called *Nossa Senhora de Oliveira*, arrived at the same time that the head of the other fleet called Diogo Ramires de Esquivel was to leave with fourteen ships loaded with [valuable cargo].

Two small ships arrive from India

Our hero applied himself gravely to this dispatch for many reasons—the first so the small ships might leave in good time for Portugal, the second so they might bear news of the mines that he was awaiting from one hour to the next. The fleet was loaded, the necessary repairs had been made to the small ships, and on the twenty-fourth of July the armada gave orders to set sail without bearing news of the mines, leaving the ship's captain, Manuel Duarte Caturo, to bear them.

A second fleet leaves, and [also] the small ships from India, without bearing news of the mines

Great was the sorrow of our hero seeing the two fleets leave without news of such important business, and much greater seeing the month of August still without the arrival of news, neither from the

Cares of our hero

There is no good consonance when the instruments are out of tune

How characteristic of envy is the prognostication of ruin

The best balance of concepts is the light of reason

Failures in public affairs are like attacks on the health of a human body

Prudence in the illustrious gentleman is like a strong anchor that safeguards the ship against the storm

ministers who had been there one year, nor from those who had gone there nine months before. With such a great failure, this notable gentleman began to vacillate, seeing himself unable to amend the news that his son had taken to court.

To these preoccupations another was added that aggravated his sorrow, and that was a letter that had come in a ship from Lisbon, written with I know not what harmful intent, in this manner:

"This business of having mines there is understood to be a falsehood, and all the news that comes from there fictitious. It was to be expected, but so be it that the best rhetoric for that which has no solution is silence."

Consider now the abstract quality of this or that passion which such reasoning would cause in all that is candid in a generous spirit, and more, realizing that neither one nor the other fleet carried further news, which would manifest as certain all that such reasoning made public. And this, and the lack of any news from São Vicente, caused in the breast of our hero that which contrary winds cause in the serene waters of the sea: a churning of waves in such a way that first they balance a powerful vessel among the stars only to submerge it shortly to its demise in the depths.

There came to mind the tranquility and peace with which he had governed for four years and four months, during which time there were no affairs, however many there might be, that caused discord in the concerted consonance and magnitude of his prudence—with which he tolerated the unsteadiness of temporal things and those that the natural variance of man gave him to drink, being in this another Alexander who partook of the venom while the physician was reading on the white seal the black ink of his treachery.[59]

But let me not justify this truth with allegorical examples. Let the eyewitnesses testify, not one but one thousand: all those soldiers who attended the waiting room filled with office seekers and merchants, who told me that now they noted not only a discomposure in his appearance, but also a change in his voice.

But now, on this occasion of which we are speaking, the currents were such and the causes that impelled them were so exalted that they obliged our river to overflow its banks and submerge its clear springs in the land.

The point is this: there is no touchstone that defines the carats if it is not one whose judgment knows how to accentuate its quality. Have you not seen that the higher the structure is built, the greater the pressures the materials convey; if one thing is disturbed the ruin is notable, not owing as much to its weight as to the extreme height from whence it falls? Well, judge in this light one who might make an ascent and you will see the weight of such consequences. Many sorrows took command in the breast of our hero when his great talent finally knew how to recognize and feel [all these] consequences.

It touched the edifice constructed by our hero at a height no less than that of His Highness. The affair was public not only in the kingdom but throughout all of Europe. It was recognized everywhere that he was the instrument through which it had been made known, for which reason the hope of the most incredulous had taken root, with four years of continual pressures and the indecisiveness

One eyewitness is better than many ears

Exterior actions are a mirror in which the condition of a man's heart is seen

If a river that gives life to plants overflows its banks, it ruins their flowers and stalks

The heights define the quality of the precipices

The high concepts; his serious sentiments

The examination of sorrowful conferences is usually the same as a malign fever in human veins

of the works and effects to which such machinations had been directed substantiating this truth. The ruination of such a great edifice was demonstrated in this complexity, and, once ruined, the weight was not to cause as much damage as the violence of falling from such a great height, which was that of the head of the prince who, having given credit to the reports, became proprietor of their certainty. This consideration brought failure to our hero, but not the failure one might suppose.

He who knows how to examine the causes will know the effects

This aphorism of reasonings and concepts is given so that the discreet and the politic may see how the fantasies of such considerations were enlarged in the mind and clear judgment of our hero. For only those who recognize them will know how to evaluate the merit and gravity of such an intolerable weight, and having done so will see how honorable his failure was. Let us leave this subject here, and we shall see what has happened with the discovery of the Quitose River.

Captain Manuel de Inojosa continues the exploration of the Quitose River

We had left Captain Manuel de Inojosa just as he had embarked with his people to go to explore the route taken by the Quitose River to its mouth, supposing that it ran from the north to the south, with the condition that he was not to wage war against any Indians he might meet. They set off, as was customary, from Cachoeira, and from there they took a direct route through Aporá, Piranhas, and Orobó. They did not pass the river of Paraguaçu, which is to the north, and they marched a hundred leagues southward through the Sertão, where they had captured the last villages of the Maracás, whose fields they found to be fertile pastures for cattle, and fit for settlement. Some troops of Indians attacked them and with poisoned arrows wounded two soldiers, one of whom died.

When they arrived at the river, which, as we have said, was 200 fathoms wide, he had eleven canoes made with the tools that the people had with them, for that many were needed to carry them all. When they were finished, he embarked with his people divided into two squadrons so that one could follow each shore and examine what might be seen.

After a journey of 160 leagues he explores the river and boards his people in eleven canoes

After a few days of traveling they came into a narrows which they saw formed a waterfall. And so they went on by land, abandoning their canoes. Continuing by land in a southerly direction for a few days, they again encountered the river, much wider and more tranquil. Here, then, the captain had other canoes made in which to travel. In a few days they came upon such a horrendous waterfall that the blow of its water was as noisy as [it was] frightening—the first, because the echoes bounced on all horizons; the second, because Vulcan himself does not throw such thunderbolts from his forge as the crash of its blows. The air was filled with such a thick cloud that its sight caused fear and trembling. [With] all the people full of fear, they paddled to shore, but the waters that now seemed to rush headlong toward destruction in the ravine did not allow them to make any headway. Some canoes overturned; some men, swimming, reached shore, one sergeant drowned, some weapons were lost, and when at last all were on shore, they considered that they had been born for a second time to this earth.

He finds a waterfall; they leave the canoes and follow the river by land

The captain has other canoes built in which they follow the river and find a horrible waterfall

They swim out of the river, defeated, and one sergeant loses his life by drowning

The people escaped this danger in such a way that there were few who did not fall ill. Their tra-

They become ill and suffer from hunger

vails were increased by the fact that the part of the territory where they had landed was sterile, and the sick people had nothing to eat but the fish that the healthy ones could catch and some wild leaves from trees.

Here the people wanted to turn back and not continue, for some soldiers had died; but the captain would not consent to it, and little by little they continued, cutting paths through the thick underbrush, searching anew for the river.

They find the river tame again, build new boats, and reach the southern sea with twenty-six fewer people

It is the Rio de Contas

After a few days they again found a widened and tamer river, and the captain ordered that more canoes be built. When they were finished they boarded and, following the river, reached the sea to the south, where this river is called Rio de Contas, well known to us.

The captain arrived here most destitute, with twenty-six fewer men, some of them his own slaves, and we could compare his trip—although of a more limited sphere and by canoe—to that taken by Magellan in the ship *Victoria*, for searching or leaving from the north it succeeded in entering by the south. And there is no doubt that if there had not been waterfalls in the river it would have been of great benefit to the state. Finally, having left on the tenth of March, he returned the first day of October, having spent four and one-half months in the Sertão and two and one-half following the river.

Captain Manuel de Inojosa arrives on October 1

Effects of the happy line governed by the judgment of our hero

Our hero greatly celebrated his diligence and thanked him, although he did not celebrate the discovery, for it did not serve his purpose. Here the happy line of his fortune, governed by his own judgment, ran its course—and it was very happy, for it resulted in the absence of shipwrecks that the city used to suffer and also of hunger, as well as the other hostilities we have previously mentioned that the inhabitants suffered, affairs that did both personal harm and harm to the kingdom. Also, the contract of the tithes increased from 78,000 ducats to 102,000, that of the wines from 76,000 ducats to 85,000; and so there was money to pay the soldiers, cargo this year to fill not one but two fleets, and ships of India equipped and dispatched.[60] He paid the 20,000 ducats for the necessary supplies for the mines, the line that proved to be less happy than that which was administered by the prudent judgment of our hero. Let us see the end of the other line administered by diverse judgments.

Let us leave our hero among natural and human dangers, [suffering] the consequences due to the delay of the mines, from which there is no doubt that the cancer that cut the thread of his gallant life was caused. It was [now] the twenty-ninth of September, and [on that day] the vessel arrived [bearing] the unhappy news of the mines together with the rocks from which the assays, administered by Don Rodrigo and in his presence, had been made to see if they were enjoying greater fortune.

On the second day of the month of October the happiness of the first line was terminated, and on the ninth, with the results of the assays that were made, the unhappiness of the second line was finished. The two lines were equal in their beginnings, and equally they ended, although with diverse fortunes; the first brought glorious trophies, the second brought the sorrows and grief suffered by all who contended with it.

Let the wise and discreet consider now the state of our hero's heart, with the bad luck of an event that was undertaken not with one but with many

The water being only one essence, it receives more carats in goodness for some than for other minerals

On September 29 the news arrives that there is no silver in the mines of Paranaguá

Analyses are made here of the rocks sent by Don Rodrigo, and they do not contain silver, and the unhappy line is finished

A GOVERNOR AND HIS IMAGE

Great events, when they are melancholy, impede the voice, transmitting the sentiment to the heart

He who does not weigh or deliberate what he says suffers deceit, and he who confides in it doubly so

The best examiners of truth are sight and touch

He who envies suffers as much as the envied

hopes, one to be of note for his prince, for the kingdom, and for its citizens, to whom the voice of four years of repeated news had arrived by word of mouth. Feel what he felt; I only wish to make it understood that our hero, with his clear and proud judgment, would feel the same to a degree so superlative that I would not dare to exaggerate it with more words than those which a rhetorical silence pronounces.

This I have read from letters written by the administrator Agostinho de Figueiredo, dated 12 May 1674, in which he said that instead of sending rocks for analysis, he was on another occasion sending bars, only it was a secret thing, and an engineer should be sent to fortify the area and protect the silver.[61] I was saying on another occasion that the cause of the errors of princes and their ministers was not always their fault but resulted from the false figures that evil men represented to them, and for this reason they were unhappy, for, ignoring the law that nothing was to be deliberated that had not passed through sight and touch, they expedited [their business] through hearing.

Thus the false figures that this administrator proposed to the eyes of our hero were the cause of similar effects. Indeed, as we have already said, conjectures were not lacking that might say they drove the chariots that had carried the false rumors, so the official whom I shall not name here might not receive the credit. So be it. But there is no animal that, when he finds nothing [else] to gnaw, gnaws his own flesh.

Finally, the consideration of all these things aggravated the indisposition of our hero, and poor health in turn aggravated his sadness, making it such that there was nothing that could divert his sorrow. I know well the reason for this, and it would be best that I say no more here. On another occasion, similar to this, in the year 1652, I wrote to His Majesty Dom João and said to him, "Sir, he who is to advise a king either must be a king or must have the heart of a king." And another time in the year 1658 to Dom Francisco Manuel, may God have given him His glory, who said that the discreet man pardons another who might be one, I answered, "Sir, the great princes, no matter how great, need greater ministers to conserve their monarchies in peace: great men also need great men. A musical instrument has subtle and slender strings, but if it does not have a bass string it cannot give forth a harmonious chord."[62] So be it.

The touchstone of important practices can be found only in the experience of great judgments

Our hero, then, not having anyone with whom to divert his sorrow, determined to relieve his grief by visiting Nossa Senhora de Montserrate, not knowing, perhaps, that this would be his last visit.[63]

On October 25 our hero visits Nossa Senhora de Montserrate, where he becomes ill

This was on the twenty-fifth of October, and having spent four days there he suffered an attack of erysipelas, as had happened in the past.[64] But it was such [an attack] that he felt certain his hour had arrived, and without awaiting further escort than that of his household, he placed himself in a hammock and ordered that he be covered so that he see no one and no one see him, as if he were taking leave of those he was to see no more.

There are in nature rehearsals that are generally omens

I believe that I have now complied, if not in the manner such a great obligation requires, at least with all that my limited abilities make possible, with the description of the sayings and deeds of our hero in his tenure of four years, five months, and twenty days, and have demonstrated the ef-

It is not easy for even clearer judgments to perform arduous tasks

fects that caused the fortunate and the unfortunate courses of events. It now remains for me to relate his actions during the twenty-seven days that he was ill, and the unusual means he displayed to triumph in the battle with death itself. Then I shall give an account of his burial and of the many honors paid him, and the other things that might pertain to the scope of this work; afterward I shall give in passing a euology that will speak for itself.

Signs that indicate the sickness of death

We have said that our hero was visiting Our Lady when he suffered the attack of erysipelas, which he was accustomed to suffer; but it was not the usual attack, which caused him to have only a fever, because he lost consciousness and it was noted that his vital spirits were fainter, all certain signs of the downfall of his life.

The doctors visit him and order that he be bled four times

The physicians visited him, and four times it was ordered that he be bled. With the bloodlettings it seemed that the enemy had retired, putting him out of danger. Everyone recognized that the retreat was a strategy of war, in order to assault a more vital part with more force, and looking carefully it [the enemy] did not fail to make more attacks. And so, with the forces of evil doubled, the fever became malign and so full of anger that, invading the veins, it gained the strongest places of the arteries, from whence it attacked with all its force the strongest part of the heart.

The enemy seems to retire but it is a ploy

The fever declares itself to be malign

System of elimination is impeded

This was during the seventh day of his illness, and suddenly his kidneys and bowels stopped functioning, thus thickening the serum and reducing it to sand and stones and leading our hero to understand that although his valiant nature had withstood many assaults, not only was he unable to vanquish the present attack, but it was to leave all of his triumphs and all of his laurels despoiled.

The soul of our hero felt the strength of this battering, and seeing the physical forces overcome, he took recourse in the divine forces without impugning the medicines of the physicians.

The zenith of the soul is the light with which it recognizes the state it is in

Oh, and how astute did death do its work here, for it overtook the weakest to carry off, as it did, the strongest, being aided by fourteen bloodlettings given him, a safe conduct for life's departure. Here we shall leave Art to execute the precepts of Galen, which treat the resistance of the human body. Let us look at the soul of our hero and how he disposes of that which was to make him exist eternally.

There is no subtle astuteness equal to that of death

Our hero was very practiced in military art, and he knew very well that with the forces of soldiers weakened and the fortress countermined, the best thing was to abandon it in good condition. Thus as soon as he understood that he was to leave that life he had led for fifty and more years, he tried to secure eternal life with good departure.

The human fortresses, when they surrender, do it so that not even ruins remain

The first utterance that he made, of what he considered was most important, to try to deliver himself, was a white flag with lettering that said TIBE SOLI PECAVI.[65]

The voice of a dying man works on God in his breast as the rays of the sun on wax

[It is a] great wonder that, at the sound of [that voice], our hero, having among his honorable deeds [the discovery of] only one river, was seen to have flowing from his eyes two rivers of such water that, it is said, it is an antidote that extinguishes the fire of all sins.

Father Alexandre de Gusmão, minister of his Royal chamber and so Alexandrian in virtue that

Virtue is the sister of Charity by being present at the call of Necessity

Only wise and learned men know how to direct the instruments with which peace is conducted

The essence of Divine Majesty is the grandeur of knowing how to do acts of kindness

The light of Divine Grace makes the most unknown shadows discernible

He who is grateful smooths difficulties like a lover

To give satisfaction is not a weakness of the soul but to equal the weight of justice with which he labors

he took his place with the lord of all Alexanders, was present at this signal.[66] To him he confessed the state of all his pretentions and, having adjusted all with the priest according to the military statutes of the Militant Church, he attempted to have them confirmed by that Lord in whose hand lies all human and divine empires.

The room was prepared, ceremoniously decorating the throne [altar] to which such Majesty would appear. He came to see [our hero] the following day, not as an avenging lion but as a tame lamb, moved to pity at the tenderness and pain in our hero's voice, and the loving emotions of his soul. By means of his minister's hands He [the Divine Majesty] approached him. Seeing open that door which manifested those emotions, He entered our hero's soul and filled it not only with the jubilee of spiritual delights, but also with peace and light, touching it in such a way that it was able to appreciate its present condition as well as [understand] how it seemed to have existed in the silent depths of the past. Our hero rendered a million thanks for so great a favor, and the Divine Majesty, who is pleased with goodwill, left him consoled.

Our valiant hero showed his gratitude by having a list drawn up of all those people who, for one reason or another, were not at peace with him. He had them summoned to him even though they might have been away from the city. And when they had come, he clarified to them the causes and motives that had obliged him to execute his orders or deny their supplications, showing them that such executions had not been born of his own will but that matters of state demanded them and that this was no reason to lose respect for the office, because the points of prerogative were very fragile. For that reason, what he could do as Afonso Furtado he could not do as the governor and captain general of this state: what pertains to the former as a human being [pertains to] the latter as a ruler.

There was no one who was not satisfied and did not grieve to see how time in a few brief days had changed the gallantry and handsome aspect of his person into a pitiful spectacle. He embraced them all and made peace with all, begging their forgiveness and showing to them sorrow that there might have been in him [any] reasons for reproaching them.

Our hero saw that his journey was becoming shorter and there were many things that still needed to be done, and thus he attempted to put in order the matters of his last will, commissioning his nephew to take care of them.[67]

Among the many bequests that he left was one to give the money needed as an endowment to buy oil for three lamps that were to burn perpetually, day and night, before the Tabernacle of the Most Blessed Sacrament, paying with this humble homage the benefit of having been given the light to know the naked truth of the condition in which he had found himself, a benefit so great that it is impossible to pay for it. While our hero was devoted to the duties of his soul, the physicians did not cease in their desire to cure his body, and before the fourteenth [day] they persuaded themselves that he was improving, a persuasion due more to their desire to see him live than to their science, for the weakness of his body was such that it insinuated the contrary. [The fourteenth] came and demonstrated to them the contrary.

Not because the office and he who holds it are of equal rank do they stop being separate matters

Life is a flower and it is the wind that carries it off

Oh, what a terrible day when accounts must be balanced

Our hero makes his last testament and leaves three lamps burning perpetually to the Most Blessed Sacrament

Sovereign benefits are paid only by humiliating the spirit and raising the hands to heaven

No science exists if the natural with its essence is lacking

He who ratifies the contracts confirms the conditions

With the doctors losing confidence, our hero saw to the disposition of his funeral arrangements and his burial. He called for Father Alexandre de Gusmão and with him he ratified all that was said, as well as everything that had been agreed upon. And he asked him to do for his soul some of the things that he had asked him in secret, from which it was agreed that he would again receive Our Lord via the viaticum.

The presence of the Lord causes both love and respect

Having made all preparations for receiving the Divine Lord, He was brought the following day and placed upon the altar. Our hero worshiped Him, and as he was very weak, he made them support his body with pillows so that he could be more upright, which was done. Then, frail and weeping, he expressed, among loving and tender sentiments, with these, if badly formed words, eloquent feelings:

"Sacred, Royal, and Divine Majesty, before whose presence the purest seraphim abate their wings and suspend from their intelligence all considerations because they are not capable of comprehending Your most high and inscrutable grandeurs, I, the most humble worm of the earth, did not stop myself before Your Royal Presence but I flew—I flew all my life with the extended wings and liberty of my free will, not to contemplate the high and magnificent mercies that You have done me, but to offend You not once but millions of times, Lord, not by one but by many and intolerable ways. The truth is I do not explain because You do not ignore it; because of this Your justice makes me tremble, making my fear greater because of the death trance in which I find myself. See, Lord, my fears are justified, for there are no afflictions that my sins do not deserve. But, Lord, when I see You nailed to that cross to redeem me, my hope is encouraged, my faith is fortified, for through Your love of me You remained disguised beneath that pure veil, a consequence of how much You love me. That and the preciousness of Your blood will grant me Your pardon and general forgiveness of my grave sins as a redeemed lamb. You will not deny me entry into the fold of Your sheep. I am a prodigal son, and You are the father of the family about to receive me. Are You not, perchance, that Good Shepherd who in order not to lose the one misguided sheep, left the ninety-nine sheep and searched for the lost one, which You then carried back on Your divine shoulders? A lost sheep I have been, Lord, I cannot deny it. But now, humble, repentant, and prostrate, I come to where You can give me Your Grace. Remember, Lord, that I also recall when, fatigued, You looked for the Good Samaritan at the well of Sychar, and in order to convert her, You asked her for water. I do not offer You water from a well, Lord; what I am offering You is from the fountains of my eyes. Let the cherubims rejoice and let all suspend their breath, in the concept of not being able to attain what they desire. Neither my faith nor my hope will be restrained, because they are sure that You will forgive me, for Your mercy is greater—I do not say greater than [only] my faults —but, yes, greater than those of all who were and are to be born. I sinned, I sinned, Lord. I am sorry for having offended You. I trust in You that through Your Word my sins will be forgiven and my soul will be healed and will be saved."

These words spoken with very tender devotion,

Conscience is as scrupulous as the light in accepting shadows

The eyes, more than the ears, are a stimulus of great sentiment

Judgment is never as busy as when it wishes to take leave of some care

He orders the secretary to write to the tribunals, the prelates, and the nobles to meet at the palace

he bowed to receive the Lord, and when he had been given the absolution, he looked at one and another of those present and said:

"By the Lord that you have before you, I beg all those who are present and those absent who in some way may have complaint against me, to forgive me, for it grieves me to have given you occasion for it. All I can say to you is that it was not because of my will; I erred, yes, because I am human, as we all are, and we are all subject to error. To you I say the same, he said, looking at his servants, if perchance you find yourselves complaining against me."

After he had spoken, all remained silent. But the room was filled with the tears and sighs of all the listeners, who, being human as well as compassionate, showed themselves to be awed at the spectacle of seeing the brevity with which the wind stripped leaves from the most luxuriant tree of life.

When the ceremony was over, our hero took notice of a heated discussion that was taking place among those who were attending him, and understood that they were speaking of the person or the persons who were to substitute for him in his position in the government. Not failing to understand this he signaled to the secretary, Bernardo Vieira Ravasco, who was the one most involved in the discussion, and inquired if he would like to inform him of what was being discussed. He said, "Sir, may God grant Your Lordship many years of life. What they are discussing is who will substitute for you in the office." To which he [our hero] said, after having considered the matter, that he should write immediately to the tribunals, the prelates of the religious orders, the military leaders, and the nobility to come to the palace the next day to take up a matter of importance to His Highness.

This order was given on the afternoon of the twenty-third of November. But since his illness was hurrying toward its finish, it seemed to the physicians that he would not be able to undertake such an arduous task, and thus they advised him. Our hero refused to accept their opinion; indeed, he strengthened his order, saying that even with his soul at his lips he would carry it through.

Our hero imitates him who said that princes, even at death's door, should not fail in their duties

The order delivered, no one failed to appear the following day, and it must have been nine o'clock when the room in which our hero appeared was filled with the ecclesiastical council, the town council, the royal justices, the prelates, the nobility, and the military leaders. All awaited the secretary to advise them why they had been assembled, for they believed that because of his weakened condition His Lordship could not do so.

Royal matters necessitate a meeting of the general assemblies

Truly it was as they thought, and the matter to be considered was in the hands of the secretary. But such was the zeal and love that our hero had for His Highness and for the good of his vassals that it, more than his own strength, moved him to attend the conference so that, supported with pillows in his bed, he made this speech, which is as follows:

Judgment finds it difficult for another to explain what he himself feels

"It is good that I have asked, O noble and loyal vassals of His Highness, for an extended introduction, in manifestation of which we are all assembled here. But your eyes and ears will be of equal value to witness the need of which I wish to speak, and which more extensively the secretary will explain from what I ordered him to write, because my condition will permit no more. Well known is the

Speech made by our hero at the assembly of the tribunals

goodwill and love with which I served His Highness and the people of this state after I arrived at this city, and the diligence that, with your assistance, I dedicated to the extinction of the barbarians—not only at the expense of the community and the Royal Treasury, but also at my own expense—to conserve this state in peace and justice. It should be known that this same zeal and this same love with which until today I have governed this state are the stimulus that obliges me to call this general assembly together, for the purpose of naming a subject or subjects who will be capable of doing the same in my absence. Thus, by unanimous agreement, people should be peacefully named who can act in the office for me until, learning of my death, His Highness can provide someone. But he or they must be subject to the same affections and love that I feel for this republic. Freely note that my intention is none other than the service of His Majesty and the public benefit."

In such a noble assembly there was no lack of that tenderness and affection that was asked [of them] to see in such a state a subject in whose hands and under whose administration had been given the royal and general power and to whom all rendered obsequious veneration. The most distinguished, because of greater confidence, took it upon themselves to render him (as they did render him) thanks in the name of everyone and [to say] that they trusted in God that he would improve. He thanked them and ordered the secretary to disclose what the paper made evident, which he did in the following way.

The secretary explains the rest of the speech

He asked their permission and said, "The document that I have here in hand makes evident in greater detail all that His Lordship has said, and in substance it says no more. Nevertheless, I shall read it."

After it was read our hero ordered it incumbent upon him [the chancellor] to voice an opinion, which he did, and afterward the [others] followed with a variety of opinions about the number of people who were to govern—some said seven, and others five. But when it was the turn of Doctor Antônio Nabo Pasanha, a judge of the High Court, he said that it should be made up of the senior minister of the chancellery, the senior judge of the town council, and the senior field master.

All the others accepted this opinion, and our hero approved of it after the secretary wrote it up. He signed it so that all the rest would sign, without [permitting] his weakness to embarrass the liveliness of his spirit for this, and to quiet the many doubts that were stirred up about such an election. The one chosen from the Royal Tribunal of Justice was Chancellor Agostínho de Azevedo; from the town council, Field Master Antônio Guedes de Brito; and from the military, Field Master Álvaro de Azevedo.[68]

After they had terminated the ceremony and affirmed it [the decision] before the secretary, all took leave of His Lordship tenderly and compassionately like people who were never to see him again.

Our hero was greatly pleased at having dispatched this matter of such importance, considering the many inconveniences that might have occurred had it not been settled.

Notwithstanding the aforementioned pleasure, he passed the day and the night in excruciating

The chancellor gives an opinion about the election of governors

The opinion of Judge Antônio Nabo Pasanha that there be three governors is the one that is approved

Names of the governors

Doctor Agostínho de Azevedo

Field Master Álvaro de Azevedo

Field Master Antônio Guedes de Brito

There is no office that conserves as many ingredients as the vessel of the human body

With precise care prudence is usually beneficial

No doctrine is as powerful as the sight of an example

He who looks out for all parts wishes to conserve the essence of the whole

The effects seem like their causes, and having good friends [seems] the best reason for good judgments

Oh, how carefully and cautiously Nature behaves when she sees herself separated from the soul

pain, which he withstood with great forbearance, ever aided in his diversion of it by the presence of learned religious men accompanying him with saintly devotions. Morning came and brought no relief, and he ordered them to go to the convent of the Carmelites to give them alms for seven masses to be said together on his behalf the following morning at five o'clock—having ordered that each convent be given 100,000 maravedís in alms. He asked his nephew, Antônio de Sousa e Meneses, who is not from this place, to gather all his servants and maintain them as he had done, paying their expenses until they returned to Portugal, and wanting it done as before, without giving him any other particular instructions.

Night arrived, and with it the doubling of his suffering, a natural effect of its nocturnal shadows, with no other remedy for him than to divert himself by having loving colloquies with a small image of Our Lady and one of St. Anthony.

It must have been nine o'clock on the evening of the twenty-fifth of November when he ordered all the people of the court remaining in the waiting room to take their leave so they could rest. He ordered the same for those who were attending him. As soon as they had all left, he called for Father Alexandre de Gusmão and said to him, "Father, this is the night when you must be my sentinel in this period of my drowsiness, for I do not know if this will be the last dream of my life and I shall enter—I shall enter into the struggle of my last battle." Oh, what rare action that our hero should take precautions against himself, not wishing to entrust such a great enterprise to his own forces, seeing that he could endanger the greatest jewel of his being, his soul, and he wanted his insurance to be no less than Father Alexandre, [an Alexander] not only in name but in virtue. The priest consoled him and assured him he would not permit any suspension of his senses, and this he did until one o'clock in the morning.

At that time our hero awakened, and observing how attentively the priest watched over him, he rendered him his thanks and said, "Now, Father, the hour of my departure is here, and this is the last breath of my life. It is a fierce battle for such weak forces, for there is no part of me that does not feel the slightest blow—all of my being is in deep pain. Give me, Father, that Christ crucified, for I trust in Him and in His mercy, which on this occasion is to fortify my spirit for such a great conflict, encourage my hope, and fortify with repeated succor and constancy my faith. Thus I shall be able to battle whatever exacting enemies might put my salvation in doubt, tempting me with that which I do not ignore and God knows." The priest did this, and while putting the crucifix in his hands, our hero exclaimed in this manner:

"Lord, Lord, now is the occasion on which Your mercies are to realize the objects of Your love, and I can receive from You those succors and favors that lead me to a sincere contrition and deep sorrow for having offended You. I sinned, I sinned, Lord, in a way that I did not make public, so as not to be a bad example to those who might be evil, nor to shock the chaste ears of the good. I sinned, Lord, not as a rational man but as a beast. If one accidental denial by one of Your disciples left scars in Your sentiments, I, who so repeatedly and for so many years, I have offended You—why

When entangled with Necessity the best sentinel is Charity

There is no sun in the zenith with as much light as that of a soul which God illuminates

There is no such diligent eloquence as [that of] necessity with great obligation

How wonderful it would be if, [just] as sins are confessed and the divine goodness pardons them, his memory might live

Infinite goodness applies itself completely to tender renditions

Love, power, and knowledge, a second time, gave being to the soul

The grace of Mary was the infusion that united human nature with the Divine

There is no horizon where the echoes of great thunder do not resound

The magnanimous heart pleases all

should I not be fearful, Lord, for I see that I do not have time to cry. If all debts, My God, demand equal payment, what, in the brief time left to me, can correspond to my debts so that they might be absolved? Nor do I have time, Lord, to consider the magnitude of my faults, which I would do if time permitted, to consider their circumstances. Oh, how multiple they were, Lord! St. Paul says that evil circumstances make transgressions graver. And Lord, how my enemies added forces to their forces. Oh, how deeply, Lord, the royal prophet David felt when, fearful of his own transgressions, he told You to look upon him to pardon him, for his sins were such that his memory [of them] doubled his affliction. I am lacking none in this hour, seeing how much I have offended You. But nothing, Lord, can discourage my confidence in You, for being who You are, You will forgive me, because You are not anymore, Lord, that God whom David feared, a vengeful God, but a God of Mercy whose transmigration was the work of your inscrutable knowledge, power, and love. This infallible truth, and having in my company the instrument of such a transmigration, which is Your Most Holy Mother, and through the petitions of my friend St. Anthony and all the Saints, assures me that You will forgive me."

The condition of our hero was soon made known in all the convents and in all the principal houses, from whence came many religious men, among them the Father Commissioner of the Third Order, the purveyor of the treasury, the secretary, the lieutenant general, and the senior officers. He received them all with a happy face, saying, "Come, welcome, because in the stage in which I am, I

LIFE OR FUNEREAL EULOGY 109

need you all, so that you may commend me to God that He assist me in such a difficult passage."

He called to his side his nephew, Antônio de Sousa e Meneses, and said to him, "You know well that I have raised you not as a nephew but as an adopted son. Live so that when finding youself in the same critical moment as the one in which I now find myself you will have lived the way you would want to have lived; the best nobility is to know how to live well so as to die well. Reform, if you have need, and live devoutly, for time is short." The nephew was touched, and kissing his hand he answered him with tears and sighs, born of his great sorrow.

Courteous, humble, and politic censure

The Commissioner of the Third Order, who had been his minister, at this moment asked if he wanted to be absolved by the Papal Bull, whose pardons were for guilt and sorrow on such occasions. He answered yes, that it seemed he was waiting only for it, but that in his prayers he had as patron a St. Bridget, whom His Holiness might consider, in such a matter, unworthy to pray so many "Our Fathers" and "Hail Marys" for great indulgences, but to bring it [the Bull].

There is no quicker instrument than the humble heart

Confidence does not suffer doubts

This mission was undertaken, but as he was looking for it, and not being able to find it, he looked afflicted: so he said to him, "Do not be disturbed, it will be found," which happened, and taking it, he said the prayers. When this was over, the Commissary began, and when he finished absolving him, our hero said, "Oh, how relieved is my spirit from that weight which, until now, had overwhelmed me. Blessed art Thou, Lord. How many mercies You have given me."

Divine grace relieves the attacks on the soul just as good health does those on the body

The priest, Frei Lázaro, a discalced Carmelite

and friend of his, tried to help him die well, telling him that he had to trust in God for his salvation. He answered him, saying that he was very confident that His Divine Mercy would grant it to him.

It seemed to some of the religious men that our hero was too weak to hold the image of the Holy Christ that he had in his hands, and they wanted to take it from him and give him one that was smaller, at which he hastened to say:

"Do not give me another. With this I began and with this I shall finish. Lord, in Your divine hands rests all the remedy of my salvation. Your magnitude is so great that I am confident I shall obtain it. Will You not permit it, allowing by the weight [of the image] on my weak body that my sins be vanquished? For they are in Your sight trifling vapors, which the sunbeams will disperse. So be it, Lord. I commend my faults and entrust my spirit [to You], assured, happy, and confident of obtaining that which by my repeated petitions I beg of You."

As one priest saw that the life of our hero was now sailing at top speed toward the last paroxysm, he said, raising his voice, "It is on this opportune occasion when the devil uses his greatest artifices and subterfuges. One must not give him credit." Scarcely had the priest finished his zealous admonition when our hero, looking at him with the attitude more of a healthy man than of one who was so near death, said to him:

"No, no, no, Father, I shall not be lost; the devil has nothing to do with me here. I have this Christ

There is nothing more powerful than faith

The instrument of sight knows matter but not the spirit

Strength was never lacking to the composed spirit

Oh, how diligent is Nature in his favor, for by dint of examples it wants Heaven given to him

He who perceives well repeats well

Great is the force of an earnest concept

Facing: Page from the manuscript "Paneguirico funebre" in the James Ford Bell Library

Pezando ella Tanto, S.º Sobre, esta pobre
Barquilla espero de mis culpas? queson · O que atiua es la na-
asu Vista leues Vapores aquien desuanesen turaleza en subene-
los rayos del Sol. & a-S, ya ene- ficio; pues affuerça
llas encomiendo y pongo mi espiritu, de exemplos, quiere
confiado Siguro y alegre deque ede= Se den dl Cielo.
Consiguir lo q. por mi repitida pitiçion
os Suplico

    Como Viese Vn padre
que ya Nauegando empopa Sacare
ya dela Vida denuestro Heroe, aL=
Vltimo parascismo; Seuantando la Vos,
Sedixo. En esta Oportuna Ocascion
Es quando usa desus mayores ardi-
Demo- des, y Suptilezas + No ay que darse= quien bien percibe
nio- Credicto. Apenas accabo el P.e Su= Bien repite.
Zelosa aduertencia, quando miran-
dose, Con atiuidad, mas desaño q. de
quien estaua tan prochimo a la muerte
Se dixo

   No No, No P.e
No me ede perder, no tiene el demonio,= Grande es la fuerça
aqui q. hazer Conmigo, Tengo á este S.or, de Vn formal
en mis manos; Sercame Su madre San- Consecto.
tiçima, y Su grande amigo. Santo Ant.º
      Co

112 A GOVERNOR AND HIS IMAGE

How well this soul foresaw the response of its divine beloved

The year 1675

He who threw the anchor of his faith into the sea of divine mercies made the ship of eternal life secure

There are occasions [when] one must permit adulation, and there are occasions when one must abominate him who explains it

The inference in the concepts justifies the resolutions

The concept of sight justifies the best sentiments of reason

in my hands, and near me His Most Holy Mother and His great friend St. Anthony. How is it possible for him to capture a spirit that I have already given to its Creator, Savior and Redeemer in whom I confide? JESUS, JESUS, JESUS, be with me." And with these words he rendered his soul to God on the twenty-sixth day of November between five and six o'clock in the morning, a time at which they were saying the seven masses, in the Carmelite convent, that he had ordered to be celebrated for his intercession.[69]

No one will censure me for writing at length about this occasion, nor presume I adorned with eloquence the words he said, for mine is in no way similar to his, since I worked as hard as I could to imitate him. Nor was it possible for me to reduce it to fewer words, because there were many more words he said; the reason was that he did not permit anyone to help him die, only Him on high. With a loud and clear voice, he did it, with such an ardent spirit that it was evident and judged, therefore, that unless he had been imbued with Divine Grace, would it have been possible for him to exist with such persistence? As if his illness were not enough to weaken the energies of one much younger. At last he succumbed with the same words, filled with loving and tender affections.

Admiration for such a death was felt by all those present; there was no one who did not envy it, including the religious. Who would have thought that the shrouded ones would envy one who had not yet felt the shroud?

Let us finish, then, by recounting, although not everything that this hero did, some of the particulars that are worthy of eternal memory; and then we shall pass to the ornate majesty arranged by Secretary Vieira for the funeral bier on which the body was placed. Afterward we shall describe the burial, and then we shall delineate the tomb, its sumptuousness and architecture, and the most solemn honors that were paid him.

Our hero was such a friend of the truth that he did not want anything to be done without this knowledge, for even those things that he could have dispatched by virtue of his office he transferred to the courts so as not to be involved in the best or the worst claims of the parties.

He so esteemed peace, having been such a warrior, that in order not to lose it he suffered from important ministers many things that do not pertain to this document, perhaps endangering the respect for his office in order not to offend in that which rightfully and lawfully he could execute.

He was so prodigal in attending to honorable necessities that immediately upon having notice of them he offered his aid. This was made very evident with all those who stopped here, either journeying from Portugal to India or returning from India to the court. And if they were people of the church, he lodged and fed them in his own house.

He made great use of that which it is said was proclaimed by the oracle of Apollo, that those who govern should be men who know how to deal with men and how not to allow men to deal with them; and from what we are relating here it appears that he did not depart from this rule.

He attempted to demonstrate that he did not execute [matters] through private channels, so

To relate events is to give life to history, which is the intention

There is no faithful one who matches his truth with that of just courts

There is no valor that equals suffering, and more so when one's power exceeds that of him who irritates

All virtues are good, but God repays none so quickly as that of receiving pilgrims and treating them kindly

The greatest justice is the greatest injustice

Justice sees through no other eyes than its own

Obligation breaks the law

The mild zephyr gives life to plants and the rigorous [wind] ruins them

It is enough to want to do good to acquire merit

Love and charity are sons of the same father

Chastity is the food of the just as concupiscence is of sinners

even from the hands of his own son he did not accept petitions, saying that they should be included with the others for official action.

He was just as diligent in not wanting to be obligated to anyone, even the prelates of the religious orders, and when some would send him platters of fruit, he would accept one piece of fruit and return the rest, saying that it should be eaten there.

You have seen very well that at the beginning of our hero's government many obligations confronted him for which he needed money. He was advised to take under consideration ordering the arrest of the contractors of the royal tax duties as well as the treasurers who owed him money. He responded, "I shall not unsettle anyone; make good what is attempted for evil."

He very much wanted the infantry to be paid before he died, for 32,000 ducats were owed them, and to do this he lent 3,000; but he did not succeed, for the rest of the money could not be collected. Four days after his death, they were paid, with Field Master Antônio Guedes de Brito lending 6,000.

Because every day the population of this city is increasing and the sources of water are few and far away, he wanted the city to open a fountain nearby, but it did not have the money with which to begin the project. Being advised of this, he ordered that 500 ducats be sent from his household, with which they began to open the fountain, and the city was relieved.

He crowned all these things and others that, being so numerous, do not fit into this eulogy, and no one could defame him in all the time of his governing with reference to the female sex.

We must not leave unnoticed the events that on this occasion come to my mind, and that is to picture what our hero did in the year 1672, executing simultaneously the four functions that made renowned, each one individually, the four greatest heroes in the world—David, Solomon, and before them Tobias and Joshua.

When Tobias was absent from his country and in a foreign land, Babylonia, he dedicated himself to burying the dead, and for this he was famous; our hero did the same, being purveyor of the Misericórdia, absent from his country and in a foreign land.

The conquest of the barbarians being in jeopardy, as we have already seen, and the security of this people depending upon it—just as with the people of God, who with Joshua had to cross the River Jordan to leave the uncomfortable desert—in 1672 our hero crossed the river of Paraguaçu and by this means attained the peace and benefit that today [the people] enjoy.

As soon as the king, Dom João the Fourth, of Glorious Memory, took the crown, he commanded the governor, Antônio Telles, that the money left in the books of the diocese be given to the council of the Holy Church so that the temple that had been started could be finished. But neither he, may he rest in peace, nor the seven governors who followed him—such as the Conde de Vila Pouca, the Conde de Castel Melhor, the Conde de Atouguia, Francisco Barreto, the Conde de Óbidos, and Alexandre de Sousa—were moved to do the work. But our hero arranged for the masonry work for the price of 80,000 ducats, an effect from whence it seemed that God worked with him and with them

There is no alarm clock that arouses one to what is present as well as Memory, which recalls what was present

Of two subjects, love him who has charity for God his Lord, and for his neighbor, his fellow man

No one is a better head than he who looks out for the various parts of which the body is composed

It is certain that God does not accept some sacrifices from all hands

as with David and Solomon, one being chosen, the other rebuked.

From only two roots of the soul are born good and evil [deeds]; if the former are sons of virtue, the latter are born of guilt

And if the above are the actions of such notable gentlemen, let us hear of the fourth event in which our hero imitated the action of the royal prophet David. We have already seen that although Francisco Fernandes da Ilha could not obtain the license to bring the royal and holy Sacrament to the [House of the Misericórdia], as David brought the manna of the ark of the Testament to his house from the house of Bedão, our hero accomplished it, locating it, if not in his own house, in the house of which he was administrator. And if David, as a musician and dancer, moved the ark [by] paying court to it, our hero, not being [a musician], provided perpetual music for it.[70]

All these deeds were done by our hero, as we have said.

MANNER IN WHICH THE SECRETARY OF STATE IN TWO HOURS OF TIME ARRANGED THE FUNERAL SOLEMNITIES OF OUR HERO

Site of the funeral solemnities

The room in which he died measures almost eighty *palmos* from north to south, with four windows facing one another, and a little less than fifty palmos from east to west, the inner part facing the sea with a gallery of seven balconies and the part that faces the plaza with eleven.

State in which the body is placed and its adornment

This being the site, he ordered a platform eighteen palmos square with two smaller steps upon it to be erected in the middle of the room. The steps were covered with pearl-colored silk and were trimmed with silver. Upon [the platform] was placed a rich ebony bed embellished with gold, its canopy woven with many birds of gold. Its color was red, trimmed with silver; the skirts were decorated with beautiful loops and silver buttons, with four gilded pyramids on a cornice adorned with loops and points.

Hanging and decoration of the bed

A rich coverlet fringed with silver covered the wood, [with] four beautiful tassels of silver and silk hanging from its points, and upon it [was] an extremely fine coverlet of Indian silk with rich pillows.

Upon this bed was placed the body, richly clothed in the manner of a knight, with pearl-colored boots and gilded spurs, a crimson cap with rich embroidery, a sword in the belt, and covered with a cloak bearing the insignia of [the Order of] Christ with train and rich tassels hanging over the steps, adding to the adornment of the funeral bier. His face appeared to be in more a sleeping suspension of the senses and of the faculties than in an eternal transition, the countenance composed, the beard dressed, and the moustache treated with an iron so that its handles appeared graceful. More than ever it was evident that it was the custodian of a soul that a few hours earlier had been visited by Divine Grace.

Manner in which the body is placed on the bed and its adornment

While the aforesaid was arranged they erected eight wooden altars—two each in the frontispieces of the four windows, and six more in the collateral parts, with [the main altar] located beneath a drapery.

Decoration of eight altars and their adornment

[Their] front hangings were of red velvet, edged and trimmed with material of the same color, harmonizing with the chasubles and other vestments of the mass.

To describe the hangings of rich embroidery that covered the altars, the purificators, and the paten—[much] less the grandeur of the rich candelabra and censers of silver—would be never to finish this paper. At the foot of the platform was a basin of Holy Water and its hyssop, all of silver, where the priests would commend him with their responses.

Oh, how nature knows how to imitate art

With the room decorated majestically, our hero placed on a triumphal although funereal throne, the altars set with grandeur, the wax tapers and twenty torches burning, the floor [covered] with rich Indian rugs, [through the windows] a composed sky could be seen that, owing to the absence of the sun, was covered with a black cloak adorned with planets and stars.

Pomp and solemnity of the sacrament

Then the eight altars were occupied by all the religious who were to say mass; they had come out of a great room that served as the Sacristy, having been with all decorum prepared with the items necessary for the priestly preparation, the chasubles, chalices, breviaries, the purificators, and a place for the preparatory confessional and ministries with which to administer the Divine Offices, which lasted continually until twelve o'clock.

Masses of intercession until twelve o'clock

MANNER IN WHICH THE
THREE GOVERNORS
ARRANGED THE INTERMENT

As soon as it served God to take unto Him our hero, the secretary, in virtue of the signed agreement that we have already mentioned, gave possession of the government to the three elected governors in the palace, who began ordering the burial in the following manner.

It was ordered that the royal fort on the beach and that of São Bento fire their artillery intermittently all day long.

Order to the forts to discharge intermittently

It was ordered, rather the ecclesiastical council was informed, that His Lordship had passed away, and it should command that the bells be tolled in all parishes and convents, which was done immediately.

All the bells of the churches toll

It was commanded that the field masters appear in the plaza at six o'clock in the afternoon with their companies in formation, marching with funeral trappings, lances, axes, picks and standards, draped and mournful drums, gun carriages of the harquebus contingent reversed, with their captains and officials in such a manner as to present a funereal and sorrowful spectacle.

The lieutenant general of the artillery was also ordered to appear in the plaza with all his officers, captains, constables, and artillerymen with two campaign pieces, mounted, and adorned with funeral banners.

It will be great misery for the soul, if it does not go to a good place, to see transitory honors [done] to its body and intercessions for its salvation

The council of the Holy Church and the other religious orders were advised to come at the same hour to accompany the body.

[The same order was given] to all the confraternities of The Most Holy Sacrament, Our Lady, and the other saints, having given it first to all the parishes, coadjutors, chaplains, presbyters, and resident or visiting clerics and friars.

MANNER IN WHICH THE RECEPTION OF THE BODY AND THE INTERMENT WAS ARRANGED IN THE CHURCH OF SÃO FRANCISCO[71]

A platform fourteen palmos wide and a little less in length was built in the middle of the church, and upon it another higher but smaller one. They were covered with black silk and trimmed with valences with subtle and delicate embellishments, with silver ornaments. Covering the surface [was] a rich cloth of red velvet trimmed with orange material and gold braid and tassels.

Both the lower and upper parts of the platform were adorned by many silver candelabra and their candles, and with loving care interspersed elegantly with many censers. In pyramidal form [there were] many silver [containers for] incense and perfume. Adorning the circumference were twenty wax tapers and on one side a font of ebony trimmed with silver, containing Holy Water. Two tombs were opened, one next to the font of Holy Water following the last will of the testator, the other in the chancel where [the body] was to be deposited in a coffin that was lined with black silk, a subject that we shall mention again.

ORDER OF THE PROCESSION AND THE FUNERAL MARCH AT 6:00 P.M.

When it was three o'clock the plaza was filled from all of the streets opening [into it] by all the military leaders: field masters, lieutenant generals, sergeant majors, captains, standard bearers, adjutants, lieutenants of the artillery, captains [*sic*], and other officers, all dressed in mourning. The ministers of the higher and lower tribunals, the nobility and honorable citizens did no less, not venturing to appear in public dressed in a manner that would leave their sentiments unknown.

Then diverse squadrons marching beneath different banners arrived. The first were six whose color was mother of pearl embroidered with silk and gold, with tassels, silver banners falling from the cross, and torch bearers and enlisted men dressed in its color. A true sign of him who, once being a strong lion, is now a tame lamb.

Then entered another six of green trimmed with the same color and gold, and its soldiers dressed in the same color, signifying a firm hope but also establishing that one who is dressed in it attains eternal glory in temporal afflictions.

There must have been, without [any] exaggeration on my part, fifty standards of white silk that entered unfurled, also trimmed with gold and tassels, with the brothers dressed in pure white, all dedicated to the purity of the one who conceived without stain of original sin.

Others of red and of the color of ashes were displayed. Who would think that in a funeral procession a springtime of colors would be seen—but who would not think it, knowing that it was homage to a body whose soul had demonstrated itself to be privileged in so many ways?

Behind them entered the cathedral chapter and priest to honor the body, accompanied by the musicians of their chapel.

After the chapter descended, the sons of that saint who saw himself carried off by fiery horses arrived from Mount Carmel, and with sonorous music they also honored the body. The other religious orders followed them.[72]

Now the sun was spurring his horses with such haste that Tethys felt their hooves splashing in her waters.[73]

Now the plaza was full of many people who were divided into little circles. They thought of nothing but the sorrow of having lost such a governor, the memory of his deeds increasing their sentiments.

The bell of the Misericórdia enters the plaza beneath its banner and crest

At this time all were stilled by the voice of an instrument that next to a banner tolled mournful echoes. Seen on the banner was a figure of Christ wrapped in shrouds, a symbol that the dead need [fear] nothing from [death]. All let it pass without interference.

Accompaniment, funeral litter and its adornment

Many brothers dressed in mourning were accompanying the bell, and at the end of their procession it was seen that six of them were carrying on their shoulders a funeral litter covered with a rich cloth. It was of black velvet trimmed with orange-colored brocade, with fringes and tassels of gold. And if this was the exterior, the interior part demonstrated itself to be a small tomb with its canopy [whose] sphere did not measure more than seven feet. It was trimmed with the same silk and gold, and the skirts and valences were fringed and trimmed with rich buttons. They arrived at the gates of the palace, and when I thought they would show respect I saw that they were advising me to heed the diverse quality of the crosiers by which they marched and how equal they were in the discharge of their duty. Thus death was empowered to recover the spoils of her triumphs as much in the royal palaces as in humble huts.

They finally ascended the stairs, not stopping in the first, or the second, or the third chamber. They arrived at the fourth and, without asking permission, gathered that which, being eclipsed, illuminated the hall, lighted the lights, and gave life to the majesty and pomp of that great display.

But scarcely had they done so when the hall, when the pomp, and when the lights were eclipsed, if the latter by horror, the others as decorations turning vainglorious. O machinations of the world: roses at sunrise, cadavers at sunset!

They descended the staircase and, arriving at the gate, the body was recognized by the soldiers who, seeing eclipsed that smile with which he used to receive them and the happy salvos they used to repeat to him, with pure sorrow turned the gun carriages around and to the cry of hoarse and untuned instruments gave him three salvos. The guns of the artillery and the forts did the same.

Now at this time not even the smallest reflection of the light of the sun could be seen in either horizon, and in reflection the night did not seem natural. By wishing to share the sentiments of mankind it did not allow the smallest star to come out, [but] suddenly there appeared many artificial [stars] that seemed to take over the function of the natural ones, opening among the shadows a wide path, and so the burial procession began.

MANNER IN WHICH THE BURIAL PROCESSION OF OUR HERO MARCHED TO SÃO FRANCISCO

Banner of the Holy House of Mercy

At the head of a procession of such great solemnity was a banner of which we have already spoken, bearing two emblems, one already described, the other a figure of Our Lady covered by such an extended cloak that it exceeds that of the celestial globe; for the latter has an end, but the pity and mercy of the former is endless.

Bell and poor men

The voice of a sad and funereal instrument accompanied the first banner, and those who in this world are short on fortune, richer in miseries than in property, with lighted candles accompanied the other.

Accompaniment of 100 confraternities

Behind so much poverty walked with zeal and divine love the greatest wealth in the squadrons of more than 100 standard-bearers with their banner-trimmed crosses, with lighted torches, the latter being the first who had entered the plaza.

The religious orders

With cross raised high, the sons of the prophet Elias, who were followed by the other religious orders, entered.[74]

All the priesthood accompanies the chapter

The chapter of the Holy Church preceded them with cross raised high, bringing with them the vicars of the parishes, the coadjutors, the chaplains, and the unassigned priests. All were given candles of one pound and their alms, which at the time were worth two patacas each.

The brotherhood of the Misericórdia, tribunals and nobility

Behind them, accompanying the *esquife*,[75] were the vast brotherhood of the Holy Misericórdia and, in the midst of them, next to the funeral litter, the ministers of the Royal High Court, the other tribunals, the nobility, the purveyor of the treasury, the secretary of state, and the lieutenant general.

Next to them came our hero and, at his head, on horseback, two captains dressed in mourning, one bearing the coat of arms, the other the staff of office.

At the rear of the litter could be seen the field master, Pedro Gomes, on foot and dragging a pike, marching with his regiment, accompanied by the sergeant major, aides, and ministers.

In order of their years of service he was followed by all his dozen captains with their companies and standards, dragging their pikes, and with the gun carriages of the harquebuses reversed. Between this regiment and the one that followed it marched Lieutenant General Luís Gomes de Bulhões, the captain, the constable, and the artillerymen with the guns of artillery mounted on carriages with black banners.

Behind, as rear guard, followed Field Master Álvaro de Azevedo and the governor, the two dragging their pikes and joined by their officials, the sergeant major, and aides, followed by their twelve captains, all dragging their arms and banners. Following them were the great and small of the entire town.

This grand funeral procession went from the plaza straight down the street that leads to the school of the Jesuits. The bells were tolling, and the forts at intervals were firing their salvos with noisy echoes. The streets, the windows—all were filled with men and women deeply moved.

In this way it entered the wide Square of the Terreiro, where a squadron of the auxiliaries was waiting, and [there were] so many women and

The litter with two mounted captains bearing his coat of arms and staff of office

Field Master Pedro Gomes with his regiment

The artillery marches

The second regiment of Field Master Álvaro de Azevedo marches

Noisy and mournful thundering with which the funeral procession advances

The regiment of the auxiliaries is formed in the Terreiro

It arrives at São Francisco and the chapter honors him

They bury him next to the Holy Water font and remove him to the chancel

The regiments and forts give three rounds of salvos, and the staff of office and coat of arms are broken

In our judgment, shadows never shorten life more than when they are the darkest

Life is loved and always desires what is most gratifying

children that, in their desire to see our hero, they impeded one another.[76]

From there it proceeded to the Convent of São Francisco, and arriving at the church [the coffin] was placed on the funeral construction, which we have already described. Here, then, the chapter solemnly honored him with music.

As soon as they had left, the community of Franciscans entered and with their chant honored him. When they had finished, the brotherhood of the Holy Misericórdia arrived and placed our hero in the tomb that was opened next to the font of Holy Water to comply, as we have said, with his last will.

They then removed him and took him to the tomb that was in the chancel. There they placed him in the tomb that we have already mentioned and will speak of again in its proper place.

Scarcely had this been done when the signal was given to the squadrons that their general was buried. The mounted captains with the coat of arms and staff of office broke them to the mournful and noisy echoes of hoarse drums, artillery, and three rounds of harquebus fire. All the forts responded with the same sentiment by furious and notable thunder, and in an instant all this pomp and great solemnity had vanished.

O glories of the world, so inconstant that you do not surpass shadows! A few hours of pomp, although funereal, seemed formidable but they easily vanished [for] they lacked eyes to comprehend you. Now a few lonely [eyes] find no trace of what you were, to fix themselves upon.

We have seen how the captains, at the thunder of salvos and drums, broke the staff of office and coat of arms of the borrowed glory of their general, seeing it vanish in funereal spectacle—a certain and visible truth, but never perceived by one who enters to possess the office. We must understand that our hero rose to occupy another [and] better [office]. This truth—what I am saying—it seems God wanted to demonstrate with signs from which we could infer it, such as those that follow.

SIGNS THAT APPEARED WHEN OUR HERO GAVE HIS SOUL TO GOD, INDICATING THAT IT WAS SAVED

The first may be taken from what experience demonstrates to us, which is that all bodies, once death has entered them, robust though they may be, are suffocated in such a way that they can scarcely carry on what is demanded of them by those who are helping them.

Death in its attacks impedes the workings of the organs

The aforementioned being the case, we should consider what was found with respect to our hero. He suffered twenty-one days of intolerable agonies including the innermost pains of stones, retention of waters, loss of consciousness, eighteen bloodlettings, mortifying treatments, no relief; his age— more than fifty years—away from his home, wife and children, and seeing himself subjected to these kinds of afflictions, which is contrary to [all] reason from whence the faithful awaits the greatest good fortune. And when it occurs this way, this first sign must be considered certain and true that our hero was saved: for in a firm, loud, and intelligible voice he ended the last paroxysm of his life as we have already described at great length.

First sign

The faithful one, truly, is the light of reason

The second sign

Only God has voice without speech; signs and figures represent His work

The third sign

The fourth sign

Notable are those things that inculcate His grandeur by signs

The second sign, although not miraculous—but not wishing to fail the truth of this history and what I personally ascertained—is what I am going to tell you now. It has to do with the coffin in which our hero was laid.

It was necessary to line it, as is customary, with a little silk; this was ordered from Manuel Álvares Milão, who gave a piece of material so that the necessary [length] could be taken from it.[77] It was done, and what was cut off measured 6 $2/3$ *codos*. The piece was returned to him and the merchant measured it to satisfy himself. He found it to be the same length as when they had taken it from him. He certified it, measuring another piece, and finding it certain, refused the money that was given him. The nephew of Manuel Álvares Milão told me this. Let us go to the third sign.

We have already said that the funeral bier of our hero was prepared at 8:00 A.M. On it were placed twenty heavy wax tapers that had been brought from a candlemaker's shop. They burned eleven hours and, removing them, they were weighed, and when it was imagined that one-half an *arroba* would be missing, it was discovered that not more than a pound and one-half had been used.

The fourth sign is what we have already stated, that the evening before his death he had ordered seven masses be said in the Convent of Our Lady of Carmel the following day at 5:00 A.M., the hour in which he gave his soul to the Creator, and the hour indeed in which they were said.

The aforementioned are the signs from which I inferred that our hero was saved. Each one can judge (with the liberty of his free will) what he wishes, whether the conclusions of my judgment are well- or ill-founded. Thus it was to be understood that God in so many ways helped our hero that he might know how to die, to have him with Him where I piously believe that he is enjoying His glory.

Noble Brazilians, the quality of the target that I aspired to or aimed at, you now see, was so sublime that I could not attain it. To put in your hands examples of the sayings and deeds of our hero, such were its origins. I did what I could, but not what was necessary. I complained to Fortune for having accompanied me in a miserly fashion, and she made me understand that she did not waste her wealth on old men of more than seventy-two years. I laughed and said to her, "Fortune, not for this are you to take the glory of the impulse away from me." So be it.

I am going to give you an account of the magnificent solemnity with which the tomb and urn of his honors were prepared.

MANNER IN WHICH THE
SECRETARY OF STATE
ORDERED THE TOMB
PREPARED

Near a place that leads from the chancel to the steps of the convent and forms a part of the church where two altars adjoin the tower arch, a space suitable for the construction was selected, leaving a place where the mourners and the nobility might be divided from the people.

Site of the tomb

In this secluded part of the arch a frame 20 palmos square was formed and at its corners four ped-

Its architecture

estals 4½ palmos high, [and] on them were four columns with bases and capitals measuring 14 palmos. Upon these rested a cornice 3½ palmos high with frieze and molding, and upon this was a cupola 7 palmos high with ornament measuring 10 palmos including pedestal, pyramid, and ball.

The four corners of the frieze were decorated to correspond to the capitals of the four columns. On their bases and in the centers were spheres and encrusted circles in the style of globes, and [there were] balls on the tops, measuring 5 palmos high, the corresponding pedestals encircled with railings for balustrades that were to be bases for burning wax.

On the floor of this edifice, coming out from the pedestals, was another railing of carved balustrades that left the entrance to each side free. Each balustrade, measuring 1½ palmos, was crowned with a capital of 3 palmos. This is the outside view of the construction. Let us now see that of the interior. In a square of 18 palmos a platform was constructed 1½ palmos high and in pyramidal diminution three steps, with the urn resting on the last of the three. This being its [the edifice's] seat and its substance, let us see how its form was covered or adorned.

Body of the urn

On all sides the edifice was completely covered with black silk, so tightly fitted to the form that it appeared united with the silk, and being so fitted it was trimmed in the following way.

The platform and urn are covered with black silk

The four pedestals were trimmed with long silver decorations on all parts in accordance with all their

Pedestals adorned on their parts

Facing: Page from the manuscript "Paneguirico funebre" in the James Ford Bell Library

FORMA EN QUE EL SECRETARIO DE ESTADO MANDO HAZER LA HESA

Sobre vn citio q̃ sale dela capilla mayor c̃ las gradas dela recolecion y tomo alguna parte dela iglecia dexando dos altares atimados al Arco toral. Se lanso vn estrado capaz de reçibir la fabricà, dexando lugar on de los enojados, y nobleza se allasen divididos dela pleue

          Citio dela Hesà

En este apartado del Arco se formò vn coatro de 20 palmos por facie, y en sus cantoneras quatro pedrestales, de 4 palmos y medio de alto: Sobre ellos quatro Colunàs q̃ con Vassas y chapiteles, tenian 14. Estas Recibian vn incornijamento de $3\frac{1}{2}$ de alto cõ frizo caña y molduras; y el recebia=

          Su Arquitetura

moldings, the fillets bordered by spaces, and in them four troops of the dead walking on palms and laurels.

Low railings   The low railings emerging from the pedestals supported in the four entrances eight capitals or pyramids. Their balustrades were like urns, the projecting parts all of gold, the outline black; the capitals [were] the same, and in the vacant spaces [there were] troops of the dead sized accordingly.

The columns   The columns with their bases were, according to their architecture, trimmed with silver, the first third [of the column] up to the end of the shaft was carved in waves, one winding around the other; and from there to the capitals the ornaments were worked circularly with their carvings, leaving space between one and another design for many encrusted gold roses. Other roses appeared in the empty spaces between the waves on the first third of the columns.

The capitals   The capitals were like the beautiful palm tree, tufted and feathered and full, full of gilded plumes, the outlines decorated with gold foliage.

Majesty and decoration of the bases and columns   The columns and capitals on their formidable bases were an impressive display; but with even greater grandeur, the cornice, with the wideness of its frieze, architrave, molding, and profiles uniting as one piece, qualified as the most perfect of the entire edifice.

The cornice and its richness   The artist did not equal so much the perfection of art in the construction as the one who, following the same art, regulated it, adorned its forms, enriching them in such a way with gold and silver in a beautiful pattern of knots and foliage. There was so much of everything that it was doubtful which was more plentiful, the material of the cornice or the richness with which it was adorned.

It was a rare thing to see how boldly death walked here, for passing through the insignia of the arms of our hero on all four faces of the cornice and the many large flowers of gold encompassing the frieze, there was no space that was not occupied with one and another dead [figure], a vista that formed a spectacle: so many lost men among so much grandeur.

Insignia of arms among flowers and the dead

A cupola bridged all this grandeur, and if the one who elegantly adorned all parts of this funereal bed surpassed the exquisiteness of his art with everything seen here, it was [the cupola] serving as its crown and its wreath that was the greatest: the marksmanship excelled so as not to miss the target of its beauty.

Adornment of the cupola

From the base on which the pedestal stood, to its peak which must have been two palmos wide, all that adorned the edifice revealed the lines of its composition, and in the entire eighty palmos of the dome's circumference there was so much elegance being uniformly adorned in its entirety, that the width of the center appeared equal to that of the sphere. The lines stretched out in large silver ornaments flanked by little ones, some ribbons of gold occupying the length of its arches, enriching all.

On the top was the adorned pedestal and ball, which, as the highest part, shone as the richest and most ornamental of the embellishments.

Pedestal at the top

On the four upper edges of the cornice, four spherical black pyramids of majestic pomp could be seen, their encrusted parts decorated with points of gold. The railing with black and gold balustrades,

Spherical pyramids of the cornice

which served as torch holders, was joined to its pedestals. On each side of these upper parts, two cypress trees were seen, a sign that such a mausoleum was funereal. We have described in the aforementioned all that has to do with the tomb proper. Now let us see what the urn was like.

Throne of the urn and its adornment

It consisted, as we have said, of a platform 18 palmos square and 1½ palmos high, with three steps of diminishing size upon which the urn sat. The outlines [of the steps] were ornamented with long silver fringes, and the urn was done in the same way.

It was covered with a rich black velvet cloth, trimmed with orange brocade and gold fringe, and crossing it was a sash of the same brocade, trimmed with gold fringe so long that it reached, or touched, the third step.

Laurel, staff of office, and sword

On it was a cushion of gold cloth upon which was displayed a laurel crown, indicating that it had been earned with the two instruments at its side, the sword and the staff of office, the latter by governing and the former by combat.

Adornment of the vault

Serving to adorn this grandeur was the vault, which, if the outside was beautifully and lavishly decorated, the inside was all the richer, because the sculptor showed great care in the detail of his decoration, [knowing that] it was the canopy of such an urn and the custodian of such a notable man. All the work, in accordance with its architecture, although covered in a funereal color, was decorated with silver and gold ornaments.

Canopy of the urn

Banner of arms

From this vault hung a canopy of orange cloth richly fringed in gold, and from its center hung a black banner displaying in gold the insignia of his coat of arms.

Four silver pyramids serving as incense holders on the four corners of the first step, and eight cypress trees in the four entrances completed this adornment.

Silver pyramids

Eight cypresses

The entire church was draped to the ceiling in mourning, the high altar and the side altars in red velvet with gold borders and fringes, the hanging on the pulpit matching them.

Decoration of the church and the altars

The wax that was on each of the four sides of this tomb [consisted of] twenty-four torch holders, in total, on the low railings and eighty candles on the high balustrades. Yellow wax was used here and on the altars.

Honored by yellow wax

After everything was arranged with grandeur and care, on the nineteenth of December the chapter of the Holy Church came with all the musicians that could be found in this city to offer or to sing the vespers, with the dean, who was to sing the mass, presiding.

On December 19 vespers are sung

Saturday the twentieth of the month arrived, and all the tribunals were assembled at the church, which, because it was small, could not assign separate places to them, and thus they accommodated themselves the best they could: the governors were at the left next to the pulpit; in front, in the chapel of Queen St. Isabel, the royal justices; on the outer part, the nephew of our hero, Antônio de Sousa e Meneses; and on the other side, the Purveyor of the Royal Treasury, the secretary, field master, municipal council, purveyor of the customs, prelates, and nobility.

The governors and tribunals come to the honors

Order of seating

The chapter began solemnly to administer the mass, having set up in the cloister of the convent eight altars where the religious and the presbyters said mass until noon for alms of 200 maravedís.

The dean says the mass

Eight altars are set up in the cloister

Human works shine for their goodness as the stars [shine] in the firmament

When the dean finished the High Mass, Frei Lázaro de Cristo, discalced friar of Saint Teresa, and celebrated among great orators for his uplifting spirit, came forward to give the funeral sermon. [His sermon] will be published shortly; for that reason I shall not give an account of it here except to say that the works of our hero shine by themselves, as the stars shine in the zenith of this extensive sapphire sphere.

Last salvos of the forts at the memorial service

They had scarcely advised the forts that the honors had been finished when all those who [four years] before happily greeted his arrival now sadly saluted his departure. Here a consideration that has come to my mind will fit in well.

Signs of fate

It was observed that when our hero entered this city May 8, 1671, and all the forts greeted him with artillery, it appeared that Heaven was jealous, if we can put it in this way, for it also thundered salvos, indicating to the earth that such a subject belonged more to Heaven than to the earth. Consider if the observation of this judgment was not correct.

It is not bad for a man to know himself so as not to swell up with pride

Up to here, everything I have described in detail was finished, and in February of this year I bound it and delivered it to Senhor Antônio de Sousa e Meneses, to whom, as can be seen at the beginning of this work, I dared with my unschooled confidence to dedicate it, for it is no news that rustics are bold.

Notable were the losses, for the ears of grain gave such seeds

In my discourse, as can also be seen, I followed what is fundamental to one who sows wheat: that he piles together for threshing what he finds divided. But the harvest of the sayings and deeds of our hero was so great that the best ears of grain were lost in the stubble.

And although there is no lack in this city of talented men who could collect them in a more sublime fashion, they do not do so because the sloth of Brazil overpowers them. I, then, so that such beautiful ears of grain, or rather their seeds, not remain in silence, once again took my pen in hand to unite them for this threshing.

Privation that impedes life of its reason is not good

I was also moved to refute some opinions that rivals, who do not reveal themselves openly, have wished to sow after this paper was written, calling these rumors news from the court. This is where throwing the stone and hiding the motive of the intention are most evident.

The man who is a politician dresses his bad intentions in courtly attire

First I shall mention those ears of grain that can build up the piles and justify the threshing, and second, although in passing, I shall refute [the rumors]. The margins will indicate in aphorisms the quality of the account.

Time gauges the events of history

QUALITY OF THE EARS OF GRAIN IN THE STUBBLE

One day recently, visiting the Provincial Father of the Carmelites, Frei Inácio da Purificação, we started talking of the happy fortune with which God had been served to take unto Himself our hero, and I gave him an account of the role he had played. Then he related to me what I am setting down here for two reasons, the first being that, coming from an eyewitness, it justifies what I wrote, the second because he authorized it.

The quality of the subjects, if good, gives credit to them and to others

"I found myself," he said, "with this gentleman in my arms when he was about to render his soul to his Creator, and he left me filled with as much

Great is the faith of one who sees well

138 A GOVERNOR AND HIS IMAGE

The spirit is life for the soul as much as for the body

Admiration depends on reason

It is not always easy for a clear judgment to define what is before it, and from this is born confusion

Truth gives life to His ascended [ones] as falsehoods [give] death

God being constancy itself, He wants us to know his works by diverse means

wonder as confusion. My admiration proceeded from seeing the valor, the spirit, and the tenderness of so many and such loving affections that he was pronouncing, and I knew very well that they were born of a firm faith and a constant confidence that God would save him. [He did all] this though extremely limited in strength, which caused my just admiration. Listen now, Sir, if the reason for my confusion is or is not justified.

"I was in my convent in Rio de Janeiro as a boy when the venerable Father João de Almeida of the Jesuits came, whose miraculous life has been written and published by Father Simão de Vasconcelos, who was a good friend of mine and I of him.[78] And while he was there it served God to take him unto Himself, and although I was not present at his death, I was informed of it by the priests who were. I was present at his burial. I saw the assembly of people and the grandeur of that place, and the memory of it is fresh in my mind.

"Afterward I came to this city and was present at the burial of the venerable Frei Cosme, Prelate of [the Order of] São Francisco, who died as a saint, [it was] judged.[79] I heard his last words, I was present at the assembly of this city, and making comparison or parenthesis of those two apostolic lives and religious deaths with that of this singular gentleman confused me. In order not to remain completely [confused] I consulted with priests of the Sacred Company and religious men of my order, saying to them: Fathers, if the dying prayer of this gentleman were entrusted to me, from what I saw and what I experienced at his death, there would be no other opinion to make but:

LIFE OR FUNEREAL EULOGY 139

Whoso feareth the Lord,
it shall go well with him at the last,
And he shall find favor
in the day of his death."

Ecclesiasticus 1:13

The words of this opinion, he told me, mean only that the Holy Scripture had said that the man who comes in fear of God would have a good death and would be filled with blessings at the time. I saw and heard this everywhere I traveled, and so no other opinion is more appropriate for him than this.

Fear causes respect and is the blade of bad intentions

Notable was the pleasure I had upon hearing such an account, because it agreed with what I had said and because of the authority of the speaker, but much more because it brought back to my memory those words that our hero pronounced when he received the viaticum: he turned toward the public, asking them to pardon him if in any way he had offended them, certifying that it had not been his will but his being a man and subject to error that had caused it. The aforementioned makes clear that our hero lived in fear of God, which no matter where it is found is no more than the knife or ax that cuts the evil weeds that attempt to insinuate themselves into the spirit of the light of reason. And so the Provincial Father hit the target learnedly in saying that the opinion that he had selected was the one well suited to the dying prayer of our hero, for he had a good death and at that time was greatly blessed.

Good communications are invested with pleasure

Evil is not in the effect but in the concept

Here it appears that the evil results wish to move me to a question, and this is not the place for it, but still I shall interrupt with this inconvenience

When one encounters the quality of the results, it is difficult to understand if the concept is evil or good

140 A GOVERNOR AND HIS IMAGE

and [in order to satisfy] them I shall make public the question and answer it.

His rivals will say that by the results the causes are known, and if the spirit of our hero motivated complaints, and if he gave occasion for them, it was clear that what he ordered was not justified. Let us repeat the words of our hero. He said it was not his intention to offend, but being a man carried with it the ability to err. Speaking philosophically, I say that these two subjects are both reasonable and just. Some will say that this is not a solution and they will be right. I shall give an allegorical solution.

All know, and no one ignores, the surety with which the stars move within their natural spheres and how there is nothing that can impede the serenity of their orbit, which gives both light to most mortals and life to most sciences.

With this said, we will see the skies in turbulence, the elements battling, the wind destroying what it encounters, the sea causing rivers to leave their course, fire sending forth lightning and thunder, the land trembling with earthquakes, ruining and sinking cities. And these being the causes of disorder, all blame the sky, saying that those injuries proceed from its lack of harmony. This is not true, because the sky is not inharmonious nor is there anything that can cause its disharmony. It appears they are asking me that if the sky is in harmony, where do the injuries originate that motivate the complaints? I shall explain.

What causes them are the controversies between the elements themselves, some wanting to dominate others, each one discontent with its [own] sphere. That is where the injuries the elements com-

Question

The good tree cannot bear bad fruit as the bad cannot give good

The firmament makes no contrary movements in its course

All that is present beneath the firmament has no stability in its ascent

One can trust everything except the safety of the wind

In everything where there is no reason, opposition can be found

mit are born. And although the blame should be thrown on the elements, the people blame the sky, which serenely and peacefully exists and travels within the axis of its poles. And if [this is] not [so], let the prudent heed this moral and relevant allegory.

In my opinion the sky equals the prince in his monarchy, and what his figure represents in itself or in his image is an honest justice, and his royal spirit does not have, nor should it have, any purpose that is not for common benefit. And so anyone who upsets such benevolent actions by tyrannical havoc (and, you know it is the malice of men corresponding to the material of which they are composed) is like the elements themselves. Some want to dominate others in the shadow of the prince or under apparent justifications of his power, perhaps giving him advice to judge another or to be judged himself by something that does not pertain to him, and other things that are not pertinent here. For this reason, perhaps, the just suffers for the sinner and the green wood burns for the dry, as was seen in the Flood when the innocent and unaware suffered for the sins of the rational. And so if this occurred in the deliberation of God, what can one expect from resolutions made by competitive men whose judgment is based not on what is felt [to be just] but on their arguments?

I mean by the aforesaid that our hero, in his intent to represent the prince's image, was the sky and an honest judge, to be clothed with an honest and good intention. What caused the injuries and complaints was the competition that some men have with others, and this example and correlation

The figure of the prince equally represents justice, peace, and truth

Inharmonious winds pull up the trees from their centers

When the head suffers because of the body there is no part that does not feel it

There is no privilege in general punishment

Kindness, like the dove, is simple; malice, like the bird of prey, [is] astute

Kindness has as its object not to err

The effects that proceeded from various causes cannot be certain

Malice always intervenes to perturb justice

Sentence of Solomon

There is no courtly dress that malice does not clothe itself in

Statement of King Dom João IV

between the sky and the prince, the former with the elements and the latter with men, I offer as a solution to the question provoked by the evil effects, adding as proof of this two things, which are as follows.

Everyone will understand that by mentioning "The Sage" we mean Solomon, and that matters of justice need nothing as much as wisdom; let us see how Solomon acted in the dispatch of the claim of two women over a child. Being so wise, he found himself so perplexed that he resolved and sentenced a fatal tyranny against the order of nature, as if he were Herod, that an innocent child be killed. By right, rivals and evil effects would attribute the death of this child to the malice and tyranny of Solomon. No. Because what caused it was the malice of a woman who dressed up her lie in such a way as to perplex all the wisdom of Solomon and to counterbalance the truth of the other woman. And if this is the first thing, let us see the second.

When Dom Pedro de Castelo Branco visited me in the year 1652 he told how, when going before the treasurer of customs, he sought to be paid a draft that the council of the treasury had authorized from the stipend that King Dom João had given to him when he married a Castilian lady of the palace. The treasurer told him that he could not do it without an order of His Majesty. [Dom Pedro] then went to the king and said to him, "Sir, is it possible that Your Majesty does not trust your royal council?" And he answered him:

"Look, Dom Pedro. When I came from Vila Viçosa I came confidently. Here I have become distrustful."

In my opinion, princes, although they may not be very good, are not very bad; those who corrupt them are men with evil advice.

Malice makes justice cautious

The same I say on behalf of the spirit of our hero. It was as good as Solomon's in carrying out justice, [as good] as that of the king when he came from Vila Viçosa. To one who succeeded in causing complaints, there will be, or there would be, others similar to those that disturbed the justice of Solomon and the confidence of the king. And if with these two cases I have cleared the good intent of our hero, it remains for me to prove with two others that I was not flattering in what I have written about him. And if one was the account of the Provincial Father, let the other be a letter that someone who saw this work and had it for two months wrote to me.

One should give public satisfaction to public censure

COPY OF A LETTER THAT
THE LIEUTENANT GENERAL
SEBASTIÃO DE ARAÚJO E LIMA
WROTE TO THE RUSTIC
WRITER OF THIS WORK

My Lord,

The curiosity of some neighbors caused this book of Your Grace to be here so long, and because of the many hands through which it passed, it arrived in mine so late; and even so, it cost me some effort, and supposing that Your Grace greatly hopes that your works will be seen, do not blame me for the delay. It has pleased everyone except me, because of its lack of new information to one who was a witness to the actions of the governor.

[What is lacking is] not so much matters of his death, but things of his heart and generous spirit, and because I hope that everything becomes known to the world as it actually happened, I wish you had expounded further or with better information so that this weakness would not be perceived. Although Your Grace may say that this work deserves praise because of its brevity, I believe that it does not, since brevity destroys its foundation. Jacinto Freire, who was one of the members of our [secular body], spent ten years writing the life of Dom João de Castro, and he understood that this time was necessary to collect all the information on the great virtues of that notable man.[80] For that reason his work was so praised, applauded, and free of reproof. My observations on the work of Your Grace do not extend further than the lack of new information, because in reference to style, disposition, placement, locution, and the adornment of words, I shall not meddle, for I do not understand these matters, and even more so since I am here far away. Patatiba, 8 May 1676

The eyes of understanding judge no more than their concept

Another cannot justify what is done to one or to one's work

Another should judge the exact motives, as a doctor the exact illness

The writing of this letter demonstrates with well-repeated words how careful I was in all that I said of the virtues of our hero so as not to be accused of flattery, which is the reason I copied the letter here. For although this author preceded [all other] censure of my paper, the reader will be able to judge that [the accusation of flattery] does not pertain to me at all. I am not including my reply, for it does not belong here. I protest that I did not pledge to write a book on the life of our hero, but a brief recapitulation of what he did as governor.

Let us go forward then, for I have proved with the letter and the statement of the Provincial Father that I have not been flattering in this work.

After finishing this work, I received a book on the life of Don Juan de Palafox, bishop of Puebla de los Angeles and viceroy of Mexico. Being an apostolic man he was intolerably persecuted by rivals, among whom was a Grand Duke of Spain. Father [blank space], teacher and minor cleric, wrote it.[81] In it I saw that he responded to all [rivals], convincing them, and so I thought to imitate him, although briefly, by refuting some objections that have come to my notice about matters that they say pertain to the kingdom and to this place. I shall do so in the following manner.

Virtue suffers, but with this suffering it increases

REPLY TO THE CENSURES OF THE RIVALS OF OUR HERO

1st. They said that the bars of silver brought by Field Master João Furtado de Mendonça had not been brought for any other motive than [for his father] to remain in the government another three years.

2nd. That when there might have been a trace of mines he had not been careful in his investigations, being too quick to believe.

3rd. That he had been too ambitious and from that had proceeded his ready compliance.

4th. That seeing his ambition frustrated with the news that there were no mines was the cause of his death. Here I respond:

No one will deny that being an ambitious man is the same as being dropsical and that the more

How easy and how daring is malice, but how much [more so] if it is equal in heart and tongue

those suffering from dropsy drink, the more they are afflicted with thirst.

How slowly and surely does the naked truth travel, and how quickly and embellished does the falsehood fly

Our hero did not have this fault, for if he had he would have claimed this government [of the mines] (for he had the burden of sons, daughters, and obligations); and if he did not claim it as a discovered mine, there was one who offered him, as we said at the beginning, 32,000 ducats.[82] It is clear that he was not ambitious: not even for this would he have risked his son and credit for a doubtful mine, nor even less would he have spent much of his own wealth in the service of His Highness.

Rivals have no other goal than that of their intention

Causes are known for either themselves or their effects. The mines (as we have described) were made public by the material from which they took form, our hero not being the one who gave it to them. It is very clear that the one who revealed them [the mines] was the captain major of Sergipe de El-Rey, by means of an important minister who, anxious to claim all the glory for himself, did not want their development to be communicated to our hero. From this affair (as we have seen) he decided to send Don Rodrigo with full authority over the mines, as a result of the assays made of the rocks supplied by the captain major.

Afterward on the twelfth of May (as we have seen), the royal ministers of São Vicente reported that there was silver in the mountain ranges of Paranaguá.

Nothing occupies ministers of justice as much as falsehood

Fortunately our hero did not provoke all these claims, not even one of them; other subjects did it.

These were not the motives that obligated His Highness to send our hero orders to command that São Vicente remit the assays to him at once, which [later] he sent with his son.

And if these ministers who were the stimulus for the mines were the same ones who advised there were none, how did our hero have either ambition to rule or gullibility to believe what happened 400 leagues from Bahia to people who acted under the orders of His Highness?

The rivals should have attributed ambition and simplicity, as has already been repeated, to that great administrator who, flattered by others, did not want to communicate this business to any other subject but João Vieira.

He who knows nothing of deceit is liable to be deceived

And things were thus because the notices of the mines of Paranaguá went by way of our hero. They sent orders that Don Rodrigo should not go to said mines but to the mountains of João Peixoto Viegas, and suspecting that our hero would be able to [be in] command, they lobbied to have the order sent to him as it was. He was to have no command over Don Rodrigo, because those were thought to be mines of greater value.

Everything of the rivals is stratagem so that the manipulations of their designs are not ruined

In addition to the aforementioned, it was said in this city that it had been written from the kingdom to Frei João Graniça, or certainly to someone, to tell him [Don Rodrigo] that if he wanted to live he should not make other assays and that he should declare publicly, "There is no silver, I am leaving." And so the instruction of the magistrate or purveyor of the treasury of Rio de Janeiro arrived, overtaking as it did the one who sent the assays. [I relate] this without [mentioning] other things which I keep silent.

This being recorded from a great rumor, the fleet arrived in which the rivals expected, among other things, a new governor and a letter in which His Highness would declare that he considered

148 A GOVERNOR AND HIS IMAGE

Political discourse of the rivals

himself badly served by our hero, in a statement that was to say:

That His Highness had planned that the count of Santa Cruz was to replace our hero in the government and he would not send him until news was forwarded from here of the mines; and that two fleets had left without [the news], and that the ship of Caturo had not carried it. And [with] the fleet of the General Company ready to come to this state, it should delay a month in order to take him, and in this way it was not necessary to wait more than the month of June [to sail] with the governor.

This was the concept of the rivals, but God, in whose hands are the hearts of the princes, filled [the hearts] of His Highness and ministers of diverse sentiments, and [they were] more in agreement with what in reality our hero deserved. I shall leave for another place its explication, in order to continue my course.

The best eloquence is that which is justified or has justification

A while back I said that our hero did not intervene in the mines as either an ambitious man or a promoter of them, which the royal accounting books, where the orders and patents are registered, will ascertain. From them [the books] it is evident that in this function he had been merely the executor, to order and to give what might be asked for them [the mines]. And it can be seen from the evidence that the things imposed upon our hero are false, because it is not the same to encourage affairs as it is to be the promoter or stimulus of them. Im-

The good minister has no other goal than to obey his prince and the laws of justice

mediate obedience in the execution [of orders], besides being an obligation, is born of the depth to which the prince is loved, and the minister should obey even when he understands that in so doing the effort may be unsuccessful. And this is the reason one must consider that the prince does not work by his head alone but with that of his council, from which it must not be presumed that something about which it does not have complete knowledge would not be proposed to him. And it would be a risky thing to oppose advice without having consulted many.

The truth is that I do not speak of this to satisfy great ministers but to satisfy those who have given credence to his rivals and those who, lacking the light of reason, wish to judge royal colors when they do not know their own. Finally, there is no weed nor bad grass that does not attempt to oppose the most beautiful wheat.

All should be clear to the superior ministers because of their light [of reason]

But let us narrow further this matter of the rivals and say with them that our hero was too quick to believe those rumors from São Vicente, that he promoted them with His Highness. It would please me to know with what words he would have done so, or with what information that differed from the news from there, having himself been obliged to note that those who reported it were persons appointed not by our hero but [by] ministers of His Highness. And if he was gullible, the Royal Council should not be so, for errors are committed not by the one who proposes them but by the one who rules on them.

The originals do not permit transmutations as the copies [do]

It is enough for the minister, in order to be good, to carry out these two objectives: to instigate affairs and to execute the orders of the prince in matters as useful to the crown as to the public good, although Fortune will decide the successes.

Neither should we blame his gullibility in this case, for the superior ministers supported the prop-

150   A GOVERNOR AND HIS IMAGE

The examples have two subjects; being one composition, one time they take precautions, and in another they facilitate

Errors proceed from causes and not from effects

Thoughts are like the needle of a compass: they follow the pole that stimulates them

For the just gentleman there is no mine like the credit of his honor

The truth [because it is] the truth takes place everywhere

osition that they send tools and an engineer. For they well remembered what happened to those of the Council of State of the King Dom Manuel, who, for not giving one cent of income to Magellan, lost a Potosí of silver and gold.

And so if any censure was to have been made, it should have been of the one who deliberated over the advice and not the one who proposed it, for our hero could not avoid receiving and remitting it any more than he could avoid executing the orders that his prince sent to him.

His rivals maintain that this affair of the mines was the cause of our hero's death and that his ambition to govern another three years was persistent in him; I concede the first and deny the second. The latter I leave, because it has repeatedly been proven false herein, and I am going to demonstrate by what means the mines were the cause of his death.

Let the truth be known: our hero was not ambitious, and there are two reasons why ambition [did not] cause his death. First, for great heroes the greatest wealth is honor, and they value it so much that in order not to lose one small portion, they throw themselves at the lances of their enemies; this no one demonstrated better than our hero in his twenty-eight years of campaigning.

Second, I can affirm that our hero spent more of his own wealth in the service of his prince and in pious works than his five predecessors together spent in twenty years. And what I say is so true that if they should ask me for an accounting I shall with confidence give it, as I gave one to King Dom João one afternoon in 1650 in the House of India, while watching construction of the new library building.[83] Recalling the accounts of the royal warehouses, he said this to me:

"Regard this. I was in Vila Viçosa. The management of my father's treasury did not seem good to me. With my own hands I created a new regime for the officers of my treasury but I could never force them to follow it. The same must happen here. However, if you wish to go to the warehouses, I shall call for Luís Cesar to admit you."

What I answered does not belong here, and I have mentioned this event only so that it cannot be presumed that I do not know the gravity and authority of the matter of which I speak. Established, then, that our hero had not the shadow of ambition and that it did not cause his death; but let us see how the reason [for his death] was the lack of mines.

All know that the endeavors of princes depend on their vassals' efforts, whether in military or political affairs. Many have sacrificed their lives for such a thing, a truth that is evident in the annals of time.

The effort of His Highness in this affair of the mines, if not military, was political, not only for his kingdom but for all Europe, because it was known that arms and officials had been sent for a period of four years; and for this reason it was an important point of honor. It was the same for our hero. For if he did not enter into it as a moving force, he entered as the channel through which many functions were being carried out, which could be subject to idle talk before the assays were made public. But after having made the great display of sending his son with the assays, which confirmed the existence of the mines, and later finding

The speech of King Dom João in the year 1652

Not all paper receives printing

Take necessary precautions against doubts if you do not wish to have censure

The good minister belongs more to the prince than to himself

Wounds of the body can be healed, but for those of the soul there is no protection

this uncertain, who could correct such an endeavor when the cord is being broken in its thinnest part?

Let the discreet man most opposed to our hero now consider that if he himself had passed four years of service, being woof of the warp of this cloth, an affair in which the credit of his prince was [directly] involved for having sent arms and men to defend nonexistent silver and mines, would he not feel it to the same degree as our hero? [It was] a degree so intense that it broke the woof, the cloth, and the loom of our hero's life, [and he] suffered what occurs when, for some reason, a new building is ruined in its construction: it usually collapses on [the architect] who gave it its form.

And thus it was not ambition that caused his death, but the love that he had for the credibility of his prince and his royal council, for all were involved.

Further back I left a page folded, which I shall now unfold to relate what I learned, as soon as the fleet arrived, from the resolutions that His Highness had made upon hearing there was no silver in the mines. His rivals had been hoping for those [resolutions] that a new governor be named and that His Highness declare himself badly served. [Instead, those resolutions] endorsed all that I have written: that the failure of this endeavor [should be] placed on the head of the prince, the forge from whence the construction of the entire edifice had begun, and that he and not our hero had to be responsible for the reparation of what had occurred. So it was, so it was arranged by God, in whose presence the most remote things are not hidden. So he [His Highness] disposed of it in the fol-

There is no weightier death than that of credibility

There are no just decrees for which God has not been the magnet

lowing manner, made evident in a letter that was sent to him [our hero], which I obtained, whose tenor is as follows:

His Highness Dom Pedro II. Regent of Portugal, 1668-83; king of Portugal, 1683-1706. From an engraving in João José de Santa Thereza, *Istoria delle guerre del regno del Brasile* (Rome, 1698).

D. S. A. (from His Highness)

Before the light the most horrendous shadows hide among themselves in order to let it pass

Heroes are like palm trees, the more [they are] oppressed the more beautifully they struggle

I have seen everything of which you informed me, in a letter of the month of October past, concerning the matter of the mines in the mountains of Paranaguá and the steps that you have taken in regard to it. I find myself obliged to thank you for your actions, as I am doing here. However, I shall thank you even more if you will assume as your responsibility to personally verify the certainty of this discovery so hoped for, the first results of which you sent me here. And so that you can do this better, it is my pleasure that you receive during the inspection 6,000 *cruzados* instead of the 3,000. And on departing, you will leave in your place the bishop of that diocese. I inform you that I shall give greater value to that service in order to remunerate it in the improvement of your house, and this will take precedence over the other services you have done for me, whether or not the silver is discovered in the mountains.

There are things that have justice in causes and not in effects

The aforementioned resolution destroyed in a practical way what the rivals had been awaiting, by confirming that it was a royal obligation to order that the discovery of the mines be continued. His Highness confirmed this in the offerings made to our hero, recognizing the value of all his efforts in which he sought the benefit of the state. And he said that it is in the hand of the prince to persist in a resolution, but it is not in his hand to forsake an obligation [once] begun.

We see His Highness do the same thing. He was

persistent in his resolution regarding these mines, not stopping until all efforts were exhausted.

Rivals, avoid attacking the virtue of heroes who in my judgment are stronger than the rocks that defy the furious waves of the sea, for the rocks show signs of its blows, and the heroes [show] no signs of your opposition. Rather, they emerge (as you see from the letter of His Highness) as rays [of light] through the dark gray shadows. It is not the same, rivals, to discourse on affairs of promotion as on royal affairs, for the latter pertain to celestial matters and the former to earthly ones.

Quality and essence of heroes

And so, matters of state take form like the planets in their spheres when they not only consider their beginnings but plan the means by which they can obtain glorious conclusions for [the state]. This [they do] by being like the counterpoints of a royal instrument, which are very high while others are low, and like butterflies that scarcely are born when they die. There were many who were undone in this manner, here and also in Portugal, the day on which they saw the resolution and letter of His Highness.

Matters of state and their quality

If you could know, O rivals, what heroes are, you would not defy the rays of their light, so as not to see your designs disintegrate. But since you do not recognize them I wish to show them to you.

Heed this beautiful and celestial globe of the sky and you will see that there are so many stars that there is not, nor has there [ever] been, a subtle estimate or a mathematical instrument that can calculate them; but the fixed [stars], according to the astrologers, may number twelve and do not exceed fifteen, and the grandeur of each is greater than that of the earth in many degrees. And I would say that such grandeur is [well] suited to the firmament, for in my judgment the firmament is nothing other than the staff and essence of all virtues. And so if these stars are in such a place and are fixed, of necessity they must shine more than those whose place is movable and who enjoy diverse aspects. I compare men on earth to these stars in the sky. The heroes are few; they are the fixed stars on earth because of what they share in the firmament of virtues; where virtues are lacking, it matters not if we speak of men or stars—all are movable and inconstant. Fortunately, virtue and constancy conserve a few great stars in the sky, and following its example, on the earth a few heroes.

By these signs you can recognize, rivals, the quality of illustrious men. Recognize them in order to imitate them, for in so doing you will obtain what our hero, the model of the sky, did: fame for his soul and for his body.

It seems to me that if I have not complied with what this endeavor asked of me, nor with what the lieutenant general wished, at least I have demonstrated the goodwill that I had upon trying to hit the target. So be it. 1 May 1676.

RUSTIC

Facing: Detail from door to the house of João de Matos de Aguiar, a prominent figure in colonial Bahia. The house no longer exists, but the door is on the building of the Ministry of Education in Salvador.

Appendixes

APPENDIX A
Personalia

Estevão Ribeiro Baião Parente

There is little record of Estevão Ribeiro Baião Parente before his arrival in Bahia in 1671. A Paulista by birth, he participated in a bandeira in 1662, and his invitation to Bahia attests to his renown as a backwoodsman and Indian fighter. He arrived in Bahia accompanied by 400 men, and another ship carried his partner in the expedition, Braz Rodrigues Arzão. Their expeditions against the Indians of the sertão are described in detail in Lopes Sierra's manuscript. These forays opened up the whole area of the headwaters of the Paraguaçú. In 1673 Estevão Ribeiro founded a town, Santo Antônio da Conquista, on the banks of the Paraguaçú as a barrier against the tribes of the interior. He later passed his rights of dominion over the settlement to his son and companion of the campaigns, João Amaro Maciel Parente, from whom the town takes its present name, João Amaro.

After completing the expeditions sponsored by Afonso Furtado, Estevão Ribeiro and his son remained in Bahia and participated in several other entradas. Estevão Ribeiro carried out a raid against the Maracás in 1674 and attacked the escaped-slave community at Palmares in 1675. He was undoubtedly a skilled commander and bushfighter, and historians of Brazil have generally treated him kindly. There was a darker side, however. In his desire for Indian captives who could be sold as slaves, he had no qualms about raiding peaceful as well as hostile villages. In 1677 he was reprimanded for enslaving Indians at peace with the Portuguese, and in 1679 the governor of Brazil claimed that the petition of the settlers of Maragogipe to raid the Indians on their frontier had been instigated by him and other Paulistas who had settled in the region for the purpose of obtaining more captives.

Estevão Ribeiro died in 1679. His son, João Amaro, carried out the family tradition with expeditions northward along the São Francisco River and southward to the region of Cairú and Ilhéus. He participated in the gold strikes in Minas Gerais in the early eighteenth century and later fought in the War of the Emboabas when the Paulistas took on all comers in the gold washings. He eventually won a habit in the Order of Christ and he died in 1721, a wealthy rancher and sugar planter.

Sources: Francisco de Assis Carvalho Franco, *Dicionário de bandeirantes e sertanistas do Brasil* (São Paulo, 1953), p. 80; Afonso de Escragnolle Taunay, *História geral das bandeiras paulistas*, 12 vols. (São Paulo, 1924-36), 5:1-23; Urbino Vianna, *Bandeiras e sertanistas bahianos* (São Paulo, 1935), pp. 31-49; Arquivo Histórico Ultramarino (Lisbon), Codice 252, f. 57r-57v.

Francisco Fernandes do Sim

Francisco Fernandes do Sim was born on the island of Madeira about 1592. He was given the sobriquet "da Ilha" (of the Island) probably because of his place of birth or because he owned the island of Maré in the Bay of All Saints. He was operating in Bahia in the 1620s as a sugar merchant and became one of the directors of the Brazil Company created in 1649 to organize the transatlantic trade from Brazil to Portugal. As one of the principal merchants of the town, he rose to positions of responsibility. He married the daughter of a local sugar planter, which linked him to the socially prominent and powerful Barbosa de Araújo family.

In the 1650s he began to acquire rural properties such as sugar mills, cane fields, and cattle ranches. These acquisitions, his family connections, and his financial success overcame his mercantile origins. As early as 1647 he was referred to in a municipal document as "one of the noble persons of the land and the most substantial man of property in it." By the 1660s he was generally recognized as one of the most prominent figures of Bahian society, a fact attested to by his membership in the Third Order of St. Francis and his election as purveyor of the Misericórdia for an unheard-of five terms (1656-59, 1661). It was during his incumbency in that office that the main chapel of the Misericórdia was built, probably with his financial aid. He died in 1664, leaving a large sum to that organization to provide dowries for orphan girls. His role as a benefactor was so appreciated by members of the Misericórdia that in 1699 they commissioned a portrait to be hung in the chamber of the board of that organization.

Historian David Smith believes that Francisco Fernandes do Sim is a classic example of social mobility in seventeenth-century Brazil. Moreover, his marriage opened doors, and his ability to provide a healthy dowry for his daughter resulted in a fortunate union with Field Master Nicolão Aranha Pacheco, who eventually became a partner in a cane farm in the Recôncavo. Despite his position in the Bahian landed elite, Francisco Fernandes never entirely ceased his commercial activities, which included shipping, sugar sales, and moneylending. Other members of the Bahian elite such as Field Master Pedro Gomes were among his borrowers.

Sources: A. J. R. Russell-Wood, *Fidalgos and Philanthropists*, pp. 186, 191; Marieta Alves, *História arte e tradição da Bahia* (Salvador, 1974), pp. 42-44; David Smith, "The Merchant Class of Portugal and Brazil in the Seventeenth Century: A Socio-Economic Study of the Merchants of Lisbon and Bahia, 1620-1690," Ph.D. thesis (University of Texas, 1975), pp. 314-25.

Rodrigo de Castelo Branco

Don Rodrigo de Castelo Branco was a controversial figure in both life and death. He was apparently born in Spain, although his mother may have been Portuguese. He lived in Cuzco, Peru, and in Alto Peru (Bolivia) in the silver-mining regions and evidently owned a silver-processing mill. Based on this experience, he presented himself in Lisbon as a mining expert and received in 1673 a commission to search for and verify mines in the region north of Salvador. Reports of silver mines there had flourished since the late sixteenth century. He also received at this time a grant of nobility (*fidalgo da casa del Rey*) as a reward for his promised services. He arrived in Bahia in 1674 and, with the full support of Governor Afonso Furtado, set out immediately for the mountains of Itabaiana with a small expedition and plans to use paid Indian labor to extract silver. The promise of wealth proved illusory, because silver was found at neither Itabaiana nor on the lands of João Peixoto Viegas, which Don Rodrigo later visited. In 1677, with the help of his brother-in-law Jorge Soares de Macedo, he received a new commission as general administrator of the mines of Paranaguá and Sarabarabuçu in southern Brazil. He was as unsuccessful in this latter venture as in the former, leading some contemporaries to believe him a charlatan. Padre Antonio Vieira commented that a great deal of silver had indeed been discovered—mostly in the salaries that these "experts" had pocketed. Antônio Paes de Sande, who knew Don Rodrigo personally, said that just as there were plantation owners who did not know the secrets of making sugar, so too the ownership of a silver mill did not assure a man skill in discovering or processing silver. Modern authors have been somewhat kinder to Don Rodrigo, pointing out that there was no silver to be found in these areas. From his requests for supplies it is clear that he intended to introduce the "patio process" of mercury amalgamation for the extraction of silver.

Using São Paulo as a base of operations, Don Rodrigo set out in search of silver in the region of Paranaguá, but in 1681, excited by reports of emeralds, he moved northward in search of Sarabarabuçu, the legendary mountain of emeralds. In this venture he had competition. Governor Afonso Furtado, always interested in mineral discoveries, had appointed one of the wealthiest men in São Paulo, Fernão Dias Pais, as governor of the mines of emeralds. His bandeira had struck north into what is today the state of Minas Gerais. Don Rodrigo, having failed in the south, followed Fernão Dias Pais, and there in the sertão a conflict of rights and authority developed. In 1682 at the camp of Sumidouro, Don Rodrigo was ambushed and assassinated, probably by Manuel da Borba Gato, son-in-law of Fernão Dias Pais. Ironically, there were no emeralds to be found in this region, but both men were unknowingly close to rich deposits of gold that were later discovered.

Sources: Taunay, *História geral*, 5:310-45; Carvalho Franco, *Dicionário de bandeirantes*, pp. 75-78; Pedro Calmon, *História do Brasil*, 3:753, 766-83; Manoel da Silveira Soares Cardozo, "Dom Rodrigo de Castel-Blanco and the Brazilian El Dorado, 1673-1682," *The Americas* I:2 (1944), 131-59.

Bernardo Vieira Ravasco

Bernardo Vieira Ravasco, a younger brother of the famous Jesuit author and preacher, Father Antônio Vieira, was born in Bahia in 1617. His early career was principally as a soldier, but like his brother he probably received an education at the Jesuit College of Bahia. His studies are reflected in his activities as a poet (albeit a mediocre one) and his inclusion in the literary circle that existed in Salvador at the close of the seventeenth century. The famous poet Gregório de Matos made him the subject of satirical verses, and Vieira Ravasco enjoyed the friendship of Francisco Manuel de Mello, the Portuguese author who spent some time in exile in Bahia. In fact Vieira Ravasco and Mello jointly courted two sisters, both of whom bore these suitors illegitimate children. Vieira Ravasco never married but he did recognize his son, Gonçalo Ravasco Cavalcanti e Albuquerque, who later became a prominent man in the colony.

As one might expect in seventeenth-century Bahia, Bernardo Vieira Ravasco owned at least one sugar mill and several cane fields. By 1662 these properties were heavily mortgaged, and his creditors complained of his refusal to pay. His personal interests made him an ardent spokesman for the sugar planters, or at least for some of them. In the 1660s with the support of some planters and the artisan representatives in the municipal council, he penned a report advocating a limitation on the expansion of the sugar industry. This paper caused a great uproar among those planters who did not share his views and who claimed that his position was merely an attempt to mitigate the mismanagement of his own properties. Nevertheless, the crown did find some merit in his arguments, and limitations on the building of new mills were instituted, a policy that earned him undying hatred in some quarters.

Although his brother referred to him as a person of "great experience in the land," Bernardo Vieira Ravasco seems to have been throughout his life a contentious and argumentative man, short of temper and sharp of tongue. He continually attracted controversy. In 1640 he had been made secretary of state for Brazil, a position he held for life. A similar office in India allowed the incumbent a vote in the viceroy's council, and, jealous of his prerogatives, Vieira Ravasco strove to win the same rights and status for the office in Brazil. He argued with several governors on this and other issues and apparently fell from grace because of his participation in an abortive conspiracy in 1666 caused by the change in government in Lisbon. Father Antônio Vieira complained that Afonso Furtado's first act of government had been to take the vote in council away from Vieira Ravasco. Seven years later the matter was still a problem. Vieira Ravasco was a *fidalgo*, and as secretary of state an important man in the colony. He did achieve some social distinction, being elected purveyor of the Misericórdia in 1681, but his quarrelsome nature seems to have prevented greater honors.

In 1682 he became involved in the Bahian scandal of the century. The incident grew out of the Vieira Ravasco family's feud with Francisco Telles de Meneses, chief constable of Salvador and a close friend of the governor, Antônio de Sousa e Meneses (not the nephew of Afonso Furtado, but a man of the same name). The governor, a headstrong old soldier, developed a strong dislike for Bernardo Vieira Ravasco and his kin. What was actually behind the matter was the long-smoldering feud between the Vieira Ravasco and Telles de Meneses families in which both sides called on their connections with High Court judges and other officials for help in the struggle. There was brawling in the streets, and the Vieira Ravascos were forced to seek asylum in the Jesuit College. Father Antônio Vieira tried to intercede with the governor and was evicted from the palace. Meanwhile, Telles de Meneses was assassinated in broad daylight by a group of masked men, and the governor arrested the Vieiras as perpetrators or accomplices in the crime. The trial dragged on for years, but the Vieiras were finally exonerated. Still, Bernardo Vieira Ravasco remained in peril until 1684 when a new governor arrived in Salvador. The old poet and battler died in 1697, leaving his son, Gonçalo Ravasco Cavalcanti e Albuquerque, as his heir and successor in the office of secretary of state.

Sources: Schwartz, *Sovereignty and Society*, pp. 274-79; Pedro Calmon, *História da literatura bahiana*, pp. 25-50; Pedro Calmon, *O Crime de Padre Antônio Vieira* (São Paulo, 1931); Arquivo Histórico Ultramarino, Bahia, *papéis avulsos*, caixa 8, 1st series, uncataloged (8 September 1660).

João Peixoto Viegas

The story of João Peixoto Viegas is that of a poor lad who rose to wealth and power. Born in Viana do Castelo in the Portuguese province of Minho in 1616, the illegitimate son of an abbot who later recognized him, he sailed for Brazil in 1640. He was soon engaged in commercial activities in Bahia, exporting sugar and importing slaves, wine, and foodstuffs. This led to his assumption of tax-collecting offices in the city, which pointed to his growing prominence. His rise was threatened in 1646 when he was denounced to the Inquisition as a New Christian, but by appealing to his connections in Portugal he was not only freed from suspicion, but made a *familiar*, or lay supporter, of the Holy Office. Shortly thereafter he was admitted as a brother of superior standing in the Misericórdia and was elected treasurer of that brotherhood in 1654. To some extent his social progress was aided by his fortunate marriage in 1650 to Joana de Sá Peixoto, daughter of a wealthy sugar planter and a former town councilman. Peixoto Viegas himself gained that distinction serving in the Câmara in 1664, 1668, and 1686. In addition he served in other governmental positions and in 1673 apparently purchased the office of secretary of the municipal council, a position of considerable influence in local affairs. He was a friend and business associate of Bernardo Vieira Ravasco, an alliance cemented by the marriage of Peixoto Viegas's son to a member of the Vieira Ravasco family.

The meteoric rise of João Peixoto Viegas is especially interesting in the context of the Lopes Sierra manuscript because the basis of his wealth lay in extensive properties in the sertão, in the region traversed by the expeditions sent out by Afonso Furtado. Unlike most wealthy men in colonial Bahia, Peixoto Viegas had not invested heavily in the sugar industry, but had looked instead to the opportunities for ranching in the interior. Like many upwardly mobile merchants, he had invested in land; but rather than sugar mills, he had bought a large tract beyond Cachoeira in about 1651 and by 1655 he had secured royal title to a vast territory of over 100,000 acres between the Paraguaçú and Jacuipe rivers. Cattle herds and corrals were established, and Indians were driven off or subdued. He seems to have established an alliance with the Paiäiäs who lived within his territory and he employed them both to defend his property and to serve as auxiliary laborers. His ability to mobilize them for the purposes of the state led Afonso Furtado to place the Paiäiäs under his legal administration in 1674. To his extensive properties in the interior of Bahia, Peixoto Viegas added other lands also devoted to cattle raising in the northeastern captaincies of Paraíba and Rio Grande do Norte. By the end of the seventeenth century the youth of humble origins, possibly of New-Christian background, with experience in mercantile activities had become one of the wealthiest landowners in Bahia and a man of substance and position.

Finally, João Peixoto Viegas is noteworthy because of his perception of the agricultural crisis of Brazil in the late seventeenth century. His realization of the sugar industry's vulnerability led him to advocate in 1673 the introduction of cacao to Bahia. In this, his foresight was extraordinary since cacao did become in the twentieth century one of Bahia's main export crops. He is perhaps best remembered for his memorial of 1687 on the state of Brazilian agriculture in which he laid bare the deficiencies of the sugar industry and the evils caused by the excessive export taxes. Brazil was rich in spirit and loyalty but not in its products, yet "what rich province of Portugal was expected to give more?" His was the classic question that colonials asked of the mother country.

Sources: The best biography of João Peixoto Viegas is presented in David G. Smith, "The Mercantile Class of Portugal and Brazil in the Seventeenth Century: A Socio-Economic Study of the Merchants of Lisbon and Bahia, 1620-1690," Ph.D. thesis (University of Texas, 1975), pp. 297-314. See also *Documentos históricos da Biblioteca Nacional do Rio de Janeiro*, 120 vols. (Rio de Janeiro, 1928-), 25:397-404.

João de Matos de Aguiar

João de Matos de Aguiar, a financial giant of colonial Bahia, had a reputation for an austere life-style and frugality, which he combined with a sharp business sense and a profound Catholicism. Born in Ponte de Lima, in the Minho province of Portugal, he came to Bahia probably at the request of his uncle, a wealthy sugar planter in the Recôncavo. He married in Bahia but left no heirs to inherit his fabulous fortune. The way in which his financial empire was built cannot be determined, but apparently he preferred to rent his sugar lands, ranches, houses, and other properties. Moreover, he became a major creditor to some of the colony's wealthiest and most prominent citizens. He was admitted to the Misericórdia in 1668, at which time his rank as a knight of the Order of Santiago was noted. By the time of his death in 1700 he had also obtained a habit in the Order of Christ.

Given his recognized talents as a financier, it was natural for João de Matos de Aguiar to be sought for public office. He served as treasurer for the funds raised by Afonso Furtado for the expedition to the sertão in 1670, and in 1684 he was elected purveyor of the Misericórdia. He owned cattle ranches in the region around Camamú and in 1690 he was serving as the representative of that town to the city council of Salvador. Despite these and other offices and despite his title as captain, João de Matos de Aguiar remained more interested in finances and religion than in anything else.

He is best remembered as the greatest benefactor of the Misericórdia. On his death he left a fortune to that brotherhood to be used for a retirement house, alms, and dowries for poor but honorable young women. Of all the benefactors of the Misericórdia, he alone insisted in his will that the young women provided these dowries be "of pure blood," that is, without black, mulatto, Indian, or New-Christian origins. In addition he left an enormous sum to provide for 11,000 masses for his soul. Concern with his soul at death was matched only by his ability to manage his business affairs in life, which was characteristic of the wealthy classes in colonial Brazil.

Sources: A. J. R. Russell-Wood, *Fidalgos and Philanthropists*, and Marieta Alves, *História arte e tradição da Bahia*.

Antônio Guedes de Brito

Bahian-born Antônio Guedes de Brito (1627-94?), founder of the House of Ponte, was a figure of wealth and prominence in Bahia. He was one of the greatest landowners in all Brazil, and his properties included much of the regions of Jacobina and Morro do Chapéu. He was linked by birth to the oldest families in the colony, especially on his mother's side, where a relationship could be traced to Diogo Álvares, "Caramurú," the first European settler in Bahia. It was also from that side of the family that he inherited a notarial office. While still a youth he received a commission as captain of a company of students for the city guard (1644). Later in life he held other military positions, eventually becoming field master of the São Francisco River area. He was particularly active in campaigns against Indians and escaped slaves. It was not his military prowess that distinguished Guedes de Brito, but rather his extensive properties. He had inherited lands in the interior from both his parents, and he received royal land grants. Other lands he purchased outright. His properties included cane fields on the Bay of All Saints and a sugar mill in Mata de São João, but his vast estates in the sertão were the basis of his wealth. These included 111 leagues of land in addition to a *sesmaria*, or land grant, with vague limits that extended from the Itapecuru to the São Francisco River. Much of this territory was devoted to cattle ranching by Guedes de Brito himself or by others who paid for use of the land. He was a close associate of João Peixoto Viegas but a rival of the other major landowner in the sertão, Garcia d'Avila, whose holdings bordered his. This rivalry was fought in the courts as well as in the sertão for several generations, although a rough division of control was made north and south of the São Francisco River, with the latter region belonging to the Guedes de Brito family.

As we might expect, he acquired the honors, insignia, and socially prominent positions that accompanied such wealth. He was made a knight of the Order of Christ and received a title of nobility (*fidalgo da casa*) in 1679. He was syndic of the socially prestigious Third Order of St. Francis and purveyor of the Misericórdia on two occasions (1662, 1667). He served repeatedly in the municipal senate of Salvador (1664, 1667, 1675), and as senior councilman he became a member of the triumvirate that ruled Brazil after the death of Afonso Furtado. He had no children by his wife, but he legally recognized an illegitimate daughter, D. Isabel Maria de Brito, who became his heir.

Sources: Carvalho Franco, *Dicionário de bandeirantes*, p. 80; Afonso Costa, "Guedes de Brito, O Povoador," in *Anais do Arquivo Público da Bahia*, 32 (1952): 318-31; Russell-Wood, *Fidalgos*, appendix; André João Antonil, *Cultura e opulencia do Brasil por suas drogas e minas*, translated and edited by Andrée Mansuy (Paris, 1965), pp. 478-79; Affonso Ruy, *História da Câmara municipal da Cidade do Salvador* (Salvador, 1953), appendix.

Pedro Gomes

Mestre de Campo Pedro Gomes was by the time of his death in 1692 one of the wealthiest men in the captaincy of Bahia. Born in Setúbal, Portugal, he apparently came to Brazil in 1635, serving with distinction in various campaigns in the Luso-Dutch War. In 1655 he led an expedition into the Bahian interior against the Maracás Indians, who had raided down to the coast. The expedition reached the Orobó mountains, and in 1656 Gomes received a large sesmaria that extended from west of Cachoeira to these mountains. Gomes apparently opened a cart road and built a number of fortified camps on his land, as described in the Lopes Sierra manuscript (pp. 43-44). A dispute over this territory arose between him and the heirs of Afonso Furtado, which we shall discuss shortly.

Gomes acquired all the honors, offices, and influence that a man of his lineage, military accomplishments, and wealth could expect in colonial Brazil. A fidalgo of the king's household and a knight of the Order of Christ, he served three times as purveyor of the Misericórdia of Salvador (1660, 1667, 1686), an institution to which he personally contributed large sums. His wealth was derived from two engenhos and several cane fields as well as from extensive holdings in the São Francisco River valley, in which he presumably ran cattle. From 1681 to 1682 Gomes served as interim governor of Rio de Janeiro, a bureaucratic distinction that few permanent residents in Brazil achieved. He left a large progeny. Two daughters took the veil in the prestigious Convent of Destêrro in Salvador, and a third married a descendant of the powerful Sá clan of Rio de Janeiro.

Pedro Gomes is especially interesting in the context of Lopes Sierra's manuscript because of the litigation between him and Afonso Furtado's widow, Dona Maria de Távora, and her son, João Furtado de Mendonça. The heirs of Afonso Furtado claimed that the governor, in order to protect the Recôncavo from the depredations of the Indians, had at his own expense built a strong house at a place called Boqueirão and had settled some friendly Indians and Paulistas there. To foster settlement, Afonso Furtado had distributed the land in sesmarias to the "richest and most capable" men, including his son João Furtado de Mendonça and his nephew, Antônio de Sousa e Meneses. These two had set up ranches with cattle and slaves with no objection by anyone while Afonso Furtado was alive. After his death, however, Pedro Gomes had sent his two sons and about seventy men to burn the ranches and the strong house, killing in the attack several slaves and injuring some cattle. Gomes claimed that the land was his by deed of the 1656 sesmaria; the heirs of Afonso Furtado argued that since Gomes had not settled the land within the required five years after receiving it, the grant was void. They complained that Gomes had not raised any objections until after the governor's death and that, because of his power and influence in the colony, the new governor, Roque da Costa Barreto, had done nothing to punish him. They wanted the case heard in Portugal or by a special investigative commission.

Pedro Gomes told quite a different story. He complained that Afonso Furtado had been his "capital enemy," and that although Gomes had been the senior field master, Afonso Furtado had risen from his deathbed specifically to ensure that Gomes would not be a member of the interim government. Gomes claimed that not only had he set up ranches, but he had opened up the road to the Orobó range at his own expense. Thus he saw the conflicting land grants as unjustified and as simply part of the governor's hostility toward him.

It is not clear how the dispute was resolved. Gomes was well connected to some of the judges of the Bahian High Court (Relação) since his son had married a judge's daughter. Thus he wanted the matter to be decided locally. The heirs of Afonso Furtado, whose influence was surely stronger in the metropolis, sought to have the matter decided in Lisbon. The incident is instructive not only of the power and audacity of Pedro Gomes, but of the willingness of Afonso Furtado to use his position to enhance his family's fortunes, an attitude that does not emerge from the Lopes Sierra manuscript.

Sources: Susan Soeiro, "A Baroque Nunnery: The Economic and Social Role of a Colonial Convent: Santa Clara do Destêrro, Salvador, Bahia, 1677-1800," Ph.D. thesis (New York University, 1974); Afonso Costa, "Genealogia baiana," *Revista do Instituto Histórico e Geográfico Brasileiro*, 191 (1946), 115-16.

Note: The petitions of Pedro Gomes and the heirs of Afonso Furtado are found in Arquivo Nacional da Torre do Tombo (Lisbon), Colecção de São Vicente, livro 13, fs. 164-73. A copy of these documents is found in Biblioteca Nacional de Lisboa, Reservados, Ms. 201.

APPENDIX B
A Note on Portuguese and Brazilian Military Organization

The structure of military forces in Brazil during the seventeenth century followed the models of Portugal but allowed for local variations that reflected the military needs and social realities of the colony. Portuguese military organization had undergone considerable reorganization during the reign of King Dom Sebastião in the 1570s, when certain Spanish models were adopted. This process was furthered in the period 1580-1640, when Spain and Portugal were ruled by the same monarchs. A major turning point was the creation in 1618 of the first Portuguese *têrço* (from the Spanish *tercios*), a paid, professional infantry regiment. The first of these Portuguese units, the *têrço da armada real*, was a regiment of marines destined for shipboard and colonial service. It was the first such marine unit formed by any of the nations of western Europe. During the War of Restoration (1640-67), the Portuguese army was completely restructured around this unit of organization.

In theory, a têrço was composed of ten companies, each with one hundred men and each led by a captain (*capitão*). The commander of a têrço was a field master (*mestre do campo*), a rank probably best understood as colonel-of-foot, since it was used only in infantry regiments. Second in command was a sergeant major, a position in no way comparable to the noncommissioned officer of this title in the British military system. Above the têrço level were the staff officers: in ascending order, the general of artillery (*general da artilharia*), the general of cavalry (*general da cavalria*), the field master general (*mestre do campo general*), and the supreme commander, the governor of arms (*governador das armas*).

The têrço structure was introduced into Brazil in 1626 after the expulsion of the Dutch from Salvador. A second têrço, called the New Regiment (*Têrço Novo*), in contradistinction to the first, or Old Regiment (*Têrço Velho*), was formed in 1631. These two units comprised the paid garrison forces of Bahia throughout the seventeenth century. Supposedly composed of 800 men each, the têrços of Salvador were usually undermanned because of the repugnance colonials felt for the constraints and hardships of military life. Still, English visitor William Dampier, who called at Salvador in 1698 and who watched the troops parade, was impressed by their smart appearance and their use of linen uniforms in the tropics. During the administration of Afonso Furtado, the Têrço Novo was commanded by Field Master Pedro Gomes. It was, in fact, Afonso Furtado's appointment of his son João Furtado de Mendonça as field master of the Têrço Velho that drew acrimonious complaint from the former incumbent of that post (see p. 199, n. 56).

The system of têrços was used elsewhere in Brazil, especially during the war against the Dutch in the northeast (1645-54). Spanish and Neapolitan têrços had fought against the Dutch in Brazil in the 1630s, and Brazilian forces had organized themselves in similar units. These were often understrength and sometimes lacked the full formal organization of the European regiments. The têrço system was altered in Portugal in 1707 with the creation of regiments (*regimentos*) each with twelve companies of fifty men headed by a captain, a lieutenant (*tenente*), and an ensign (*alferes*). The regiment was commanded by a colonel, a lieutenant colonel (*tenente coronel*), and a sergeant major (*sargento mór*). This regimental organization was instituted in Brazil in 1749-50, but to some extent it had long existed among the militia and irregular troops in the colony.

In truth, much of the soldiering in Brazil had been done not by the paid têrços but by the *ordenanças* or militia forces. In theory, all able-bodied men ages fifteen to sixty were subject to military service, with exceptions for certain occupations and privileged groups. Provisions for a colonial home guard were made in the early sixteenth century, and by the 1550s some form of militia organization existed. Each town or region was required to form as many companies as its population warranted. By 1612 the Recôncavo of Bahia was capable of fielding twelve companies of militia. In 1668 four ordenanças were created in Bahia along European lines. The ordenanças, sometimes called "troops of the second line," were, in Brazil, actually the first line of defense and carried the brunt of most campaigns.

There was considerable variation in the structure of the ordenanças from captaincy to captaincy and over time. The basic form had been set forth in the regulations of the captain majors (*capitães mores*) of 1570. Usually each parish fielded a company nominally made up of 250 men led by a captain. A variable number of companies were commanded by a captain major and his second in command, a sergeant major (*sargento mór*). In some places colonels were appointed to lead larger units made up of four or more ordenanças.

In addition, social realities of the Brazilian colony produced other military forces. Groups of Indians were sometimes organized into military contingents in times of crisis and more commonly were used as shock troops against other Indians or runaway slaves. Regiments of black and mulatto troops called the "Henriques" (after Henrique Dias, a black leader against the Dutch) were created in many places in Brazil and flourished especially in the eighteenth century. These were often used for such semipolice functions as the destruction of runaway-slave communities.

Aspects of formal military organization were adapted selectively by the semimilitary expeditions organized privately or by the state for exploration, suppression of hostile Indians, or the search for mineral wealth. A leader usually took the title of *capitão-mór* (captain major). He was assisted by captains and group leaders (*cabos da esquadra*). Expeditions usually had a chaplain and often a notary or secretary. In special instances commanders of such expeditions, or bandeiras, received commissions from royal officials or town councils. Titles such as "captain of the Conquest of the Barbarians" were of this ad hoc nature.

During the colonial period many governors and viceroys who ruled Brazil were, like Afonso Furtado, experienced military men. In times of crisis, Luso-Brazilian troops acquitted themselves well as their victories over the Dutch in the northeast and later over the Spanish in the Rio de la Plata testify. Colonial troops were especially effective in the bush warfare and guerrilla tactics of campaigns against hostile Indians or European rivals in the interior. Despite the image that Lopes Sierra presents of a highly militarized society, the reader should not be misled. Garrisons were often unpaid and undermanned. One governor complained that the only men who enlisted in Brazil were children of the poor, who upon reaching puberty were ashamed of going about without clothes and thus enlisted to have food, clothing, and a place to live. After ten years, when they had reached an age and level of experience that would make them useful, most spent their time trying to desert.[1] Earlier, in 1720, King Dom João V noted he had been informed that the "repugnance that the sons of Brazil have toward the occupation of soldier is incredible, for no other reason than the great liberty in which they live."[2] Such complaints were voiced throughout the colonial period. For the planters and ranchers, however, a commission in the ordenanças was prized as a mark of social distinction and sometimes as a substitute for nobility.

Sources: This appendix is based on a number of sources including Luís Monteiro da Costa, *Na Bahia Colonial* (Salvador, no date); *História do exército brasileiro*, 3 vols. (Brasilia, 1972). Especially useful are the works of Portuguese historian Gastão de Mello de Matos, including his entries on the army, artillery, and militia in the *Dicionário de história de Portugal*, 4 vols. (Lisbon, 1963-71). See also his *Notícias do têrço da armada real, 1618-1707* (Lisbon, 1932). On the military organization of the bandeiras see Ricardo Roman Blanco, *Las "Bandeiras"* (Brasilia, 1966). Also useful is Geoffrey Parker, *The Army of Flanders and the Spanish Road, 1567-1659* (Cambridge, 1972). See also José Maria Latino Coelho, *História militar e política de Portugal*, 3 vols. (Lisbon, 1891).

Notes

1. Governor of Bahia to the Overseas Council (25 September 1761), Instituto Histórico e Geográfico Brasileiro, Arquivo 1.1.14.

2. King to Governor Vasco Fernandes Cesar de Meneses (18 March 1720), Arquivo Público do Estado da Bahia (Salvador), Ordens regias 20, n.37.

APPENDIX C
Genealogy of Afonso Furtado, Viscount of Barbacena

Escutcheon of viscounts of Barbacena with the arms of the Castros do Rio and Mendonças; adapted from the mansion of the Barbacenas in the Campo de Santa Clara, Lisbon.

Genealogy of Afonso Furtado, Viscount of Barbacena

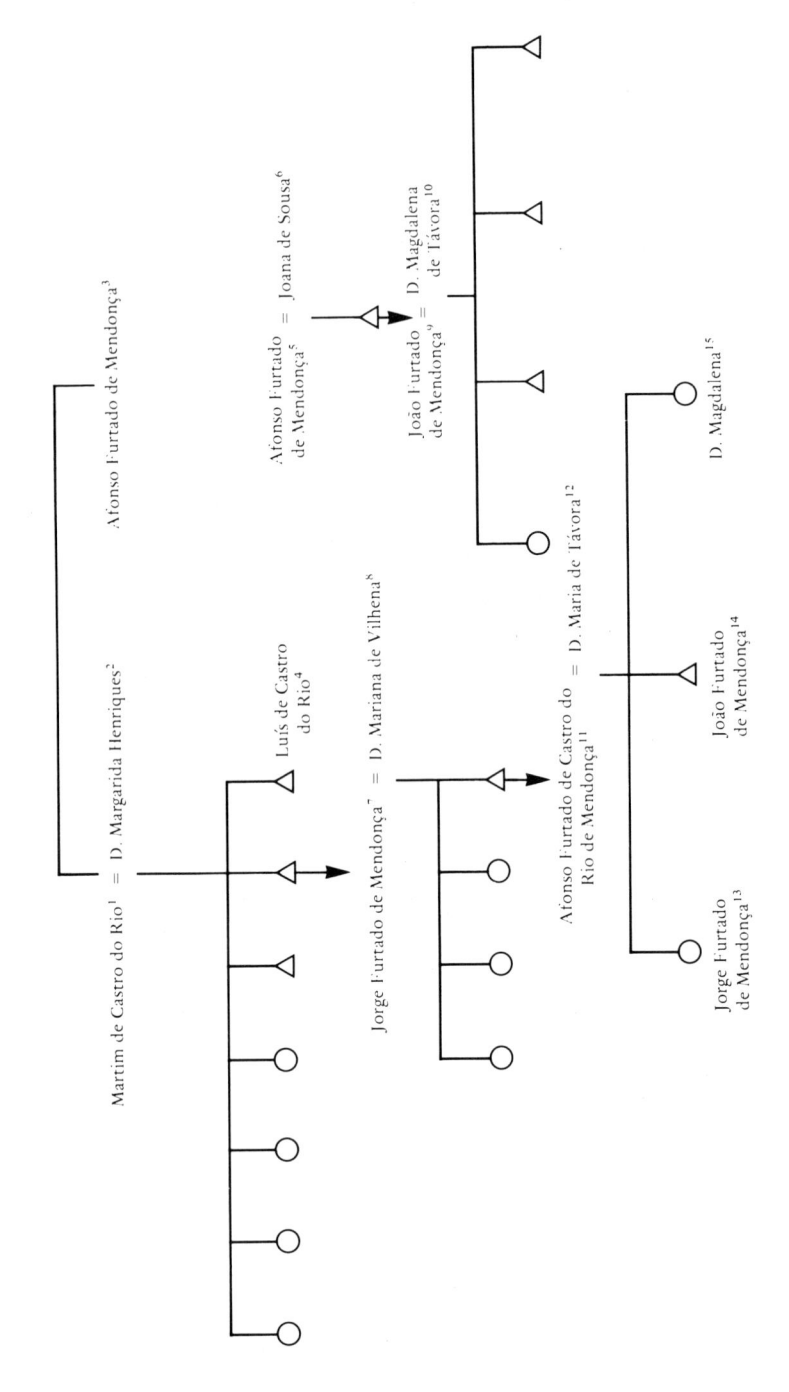

Martim de Castro do Rio[1] = D. Margarida Henriques[2]

Afonso Furtado de Mendonça[3]

Luís de Castro do Rio[4]

Afonso Furtado de Mendonça[5] = Joana de Sousa[6]

Jorge Furtado de Mendonça[7] = D. Mariana de Vilhena[8]

João Furtado de Mendonça[9] = D. Magdalena de Távora[10]

Afonso Furtado de Castro do Rio de Mendonça[11] = D. Maria de Távora[12]

Jorge Furtado de Mendonça[13]

João Furtado de Mendonça[14]

D. Magdalena[15]

[1] Second lord of Barbacena; died in 1613.

[2] Descendant of Martim Afonso de Sousa, lord of Mortágua.

[3] Archbishop of Lisbon and an important figure in the period of the Iberian union. Served as one of the governors of Portugal; died in 1630. See Arquivo Nacional da Torre do Tombo (Lisbon), *Santo Oficio, habilitação*, maço 1, n. 11.

[4] Third lord of Barbacena, Commander of the Order of Christ, constable-major (alcaide-mór) of Covilhã. Married twice but left no heirs. Lordship of Barbacena passed, therefore, to his brother Jorge (n. 7).

[5] There may have been a direct relationship between this Afonso Furtado de Mendonça and the family associated with Barbacena, but the standard genealogies do not make this relationship clear.

[6] Daughter of Dr. Alvaro Fernandes, chancellor of the king, Dom Manuel.

[7] Fourth lord of Barbacena, Commander of the Order of Christ, constable-maior of Covilhã.

[8] Daughter of Ayres Telles da Silva. Her husband was her first cousin. Her great-grandfather was D. Francisco de Sousa, lord of Beringel and governor of Brazil, 1591-1602.

[9] Had a distinguished career in royal service. Served as governor of Angola (1594-1602), as president of the Câmara de Lisbon, as a member of the Council of Portugal, and as president of the Council of India.

[10] Daughter of Álvaro de Sousa, who had soldiered for many years in India and who eventually served on the Council of Portugal under Philip II. Mother was Dona Francisca de Távora, sister of Dom Cristovão de Moura, Philip II's primary supporter in Portugal and his viceroy there from 1600-1603 and from 1608-11.

[11] First viscount of Barbacena, Commander in the Order of Christ, governor of arms of Beira, member of the Council of War, governor of Brazil, 1671-75.

[12] Among her brothers and sisters: António de Mendonça, knight of Malta and field master in Flanders; André Furtado de Mendonça, bishop of Miranda; Francisca de Mendonça, who married Luís de Miranda de Henriques Pinto, governor of Madeira (1636-40).

[13] Second viscount of Barbacena, governor of arms of Beira during the War of the Spanish Succession. He married, in Heidelberg, Dona Ana Luisa, daughter of the count of Hohenloe.

[14] Governor of Rio de Janeiro (1686-89). Served in military posts in the War of Restoration and in Brazil.

[15] His only daughter. She never married, and entered a convent in Portugal.

APPENDIX D
Weights, Measures, and Currency

Weights and measures used in the "Paneguirico funebre" are confusing because the author used both Spanish and Portuguese standards. Another problem faced by historians of colonial Brazil is that regional measures often varied considerably from the Lisbon standard. Where possible, the accepted usage of Bahia has been employed throughout. The following terms are found in the text or are helpful in understanding the ratios of measurement. All are Portuguese units unless otherwise noted.

Measures of Length

legua (league) = between 5,555 and 6,600 meters
braça (fathom) = 2.20 meters
vara (yard) = 1.10 meters
palmo (span) = .22 meter

Spanish
codo (cubit) = .46 to .56 meter

Measures of Dry Capacity

alqueire (approx. 1 English bushel) = 36.27 liters

Weights

quintal (corresponds to English hundredweight) = 59.98 kilos
arroba = 14.75 kilos
arratel or *libra* (corresponds to English pound) = .46 kilo

Spanish

arroba = 11.36 kilos
adarme = 1,797 grams

Currency

1 *real* (plural, *réis*) = basic monetary unit
400 *réis* = 1 *cruzado* (common silver coin)
600 *réis* = 1 *pataca*
1000 *réis* = 1 *milréis*

Spanish

1 *maravedí* = basic monetary unit
34 *maravedís* = 1 *real*
272 *maravedís* or 8 *reales* = 1 *real de ocho* (also called *peso fuerte*)
375 *maravedís* = 1 *ducado de plata* (ducat)

Note: In colonial Brazil the currency of Spanish America, especially the silver coins minted in Peru, circulated widely. The "piece of eight" (*real de ocho*) was called a *pataca* in Brazil. Its value varied considerably over time because Portuguese currency was devalued owing to a shortage of metal and the pressures of war from 1640 to 1668. In 1600 the *pataca* was equal to 360 *réis*; in 1643 its value was 480 *réis*; in 1668 it rose to 600 *réis*; and by 1679 the *pataca* was valued at 640 *réis*. During the administration of Afonso Furtado in Bahia, the Portuguese *milréis* was equal to 1.6 *pesos fuertes* (*reales de ocho*). In more comparative terms, in 1676 £100 sterling was equal to 293.22 *milréis*, or 469.15 *pesos fuertes*.

Notes

Abbreviations

Archival

AHU	Arquivo Histórico Ultramarino (Lisbon)
ANRJ	Arquivo Nacional de Rio de Janeiro
ANTT	Arquivo Nacional da Torre do Tombo (Lisbon)
APB	Arquivo Público do Estado da Bahia (Salvador)
ASCMB	Arquivo da Santa Casa da Misericórdia da Bahia
IHGB	Instituto Histórico e Geográfico Brasileiro (Rio de Janeiro)
PRO	Public Record Office (London)

Printed

AAPB	*Anais do Arquivo Público da Bahia*
ACMS	*Atas da Câmara. Documentos históricos do Arquivo Municipal* (Salvador, 1949-)
DBSB	Francisco de Assis Carvalho Franco, *Dicionário de bandeirantes e sertanistas do Brasil* (São Paulo, 1953)
DHBNR	*Documentos históricos da Biblioteca Nacional do Rio de Janeiro*, 120 vols. (Rio de Janeiro, 1928-)
DHP	*Dicionário de história de Portugal*, 4 vols., edited by Joel Serrão (Lisbon, 1963-71)
HCJB	Serafim Leite, *História da Companhia de Jesus no Brasil*, 10 vols. (Lisbon, 1938-50)
HGBP	Afonso de Escragnolle Taunay, *História geral das bandeiras paulistas*, 12 vols. (São Paulo, 1924-36)
MHPB	Ignácio Accioli de Cerqueira e Silva, *Memorias historicas e politicas da Bahia*, 6 vols., edited by Bras do Amaral (Bahia, 1919-40)

NOTES

NOTES TO THE INTRODUCTION

1. The process of early Portuguese-Indian contacts in Brazil is summarized in Stuart B. Schwartz, "Indian Labor and New World Plantations: European Demands and Indian Responses in Northeastern Brazil," *American Historical Review* 83:1 (February 1978), 43-79. See also John Hemming, *Red Gold. The Destruction of the Brazilian Indians* (Cambridge, Mass., 1977).

2. Gabriel Dellon, *A Voyage to the East Indies*, trans. from French (London, 1698), pp. 201-2. For an adequate description of Bahia in this period, based on primary sources, see José Pinheiro da Silva, "A capitania da Baía. Subsidios para a história da sua colonização na 2ª metade do século XVII," *Revista Portuguesa de História* 7 (1959): 44-284; 9 (1960): 211-45.

3. This is the present town of Itaporá on the Paraguaçu River, in the "campos de Aporá," and not the modern town of Aporá north of Salvador.

4. A detailed account of the Indian wars is presented in the report of the *mesa grande*, or plenary session, of the High Court (4 March 1669). APB, *Ordens regias* 30.

5. Afonso de E. Taunay, *História geral das bandeiras paulistas*, 11 vols. (São Paulo, 1924-50), 4:320-68; 5:3-40; (hereafter Taunay, *HGBP*). Urbino Vianna, *Bandeiras e sertanistas bahianos* (São Paulo, 1935), pp. 32-45.

6. João Peixoto Viegas had established a close relatonship with the Paiäiäs, whom he used as protection for his ranches and as labor. He brought them to the service of Estevão Ribeiro Baião Parente and he received in 1674 the title of Administrator of the Indians of the Paiäiä nation. See the document in Ignácio Accioli de Cerqueira e Silva, *Memorias historicas e politicas*, annotated by Braz do Amaral, 6 vols. (Bahia, 1940), 2:230-33. See also the short biography in Appendix A of this volume.

7. Several relevant documents are reprinted in Accioli, *Memorias historicas*, 2:230-34, 287. See also Taunay, *HGBP*, 5:3-36.

8. Taunay was forced to admit that because of the missing documents in the São Paulo register for the years 1672-77: "For this reason we did not advance in any way

that which is already well-known in respect to this great glory won in Bahia by that Paulista expedition." Taunay, *HGBP*, 4:367-68. For a short account in English see Hemming, *Red Gold*, pp. 346-51, 612-13.

9. The early expeditions are summarized in Pedro Calmon, *O segredo das minas da prata* (Rio de Janeiro, 1950). See also "Penetração das terras bahianas," *Anais do Arquivo Público da Bahia*, ano 4 (1920), v. 6-7 (hereafter, *AAPB*). Stuart B. Schwartz, *Sovereignty and Society in Colonial Brazil* (Berkeley, 1973), pp. 122, 139, discusses the search for mines in the late sixteenth and early seventeenth centuries.

10. Taunay, *HGBP*, 7:128, 5:313.

11. Ward Barrett and Stuart B. Schwartz, "Comparación entre dos economias azucareras coloniales: Morelos, México y Bahia, Brasil," in Enrique Florescano, ed., *Haciendas, latifundios, y plantaciones en América Latina* (Mexico, 1975), pp. 532-72.

12. Letter of the Câmara of Bahia (24 August 1672), AHU, Bahia *papéis avulsos*, caixa 13, 1st series uncataloged; AHU Codice 252, f. 5.

13. Wanderley Pinho, *História de um engenho no Recôncavo* (Rio de Janeiro, 1951), pp. 194-95.

14. Vitorino Magalhães Godinho, *Ensaios*, 3 vols. (Lisbon, 1968-), 2:293-315.

15. On various administrative reforms see Mario Rodriguez, "Dom Pedro de Bragança and Colônia do Sacramento, 1680-1705," *Hispanic American Historical Review* 38 (May 1958): 179-208.

16. The literature on this topic is vast. For an introduction see Sérgio Buarque de Holanda, *Visão do paraiso* (Rio de Janeiro, 1959).

17. Alice P. Canabrava, *O comércio português no Rio da Prata, 1580-1640* (São Paulo, 1944).

18. A. de Magalhães Basto, ed., *Viagem de Francisco Pyrard de Laval*, translated by Joaquim Heliodoro da Cunha Rivara (Oporto, 1944).

19. See Eric Axelson, *Portuguese in South-East Africa, 1600-1700* (Johannesburg, 1960), pp. 129-44.

20. An excellent survey of the Portuguese movements in southern Brazil is contained in Dauril Alden, *Royal Government in Colonial Brazil* (Berkeley, 1968), pp. 59-116.

21. *Alvará*, ANTT, Chancelaria Ordem de Cristo, Livro 23, ff. 52-53.

22. The documents of purchase as well as a brief discussion of the seigneurial rights to Barbacena are found in Joaquim Dias Barroso, *Os Motins em Barbacena* (Elvas, 1899), pp. 52-55.

23. ANTT, Chancelaria Ordem de Cristo, Livro 36, f. 154. He received at this time the right to be invested as a knight by any professed knight of the Order in either Lisbon or Covilhã.

24. Conde de Ericeira, *História de Portugal Restaurado*, 4 vols. (Oporto, 1946), 3:34, 232. The highest ranks in the Portuguese army of Restoration were, in descending order: governor of arms (*governador das armas*), field master general (*mestre do campo general*), general of cavalry (*general da cavalaria*), and general of artillery (*general da artilleria*).

25. *Alvará* (28 April 1660), Tombo da Casa de Barbacena, f. 42v., reprinted in Dias Barroso, *Os Motins*, pp. 51-53n.

26. Aside from the Count of Ericeira's classic history of the war, the editor has drawn information concerning Afonso Furtado's military activities from the following docu-

ments: ANTT, Chancelaria Afonso VI, Doações, Livro 41, f. 12 (16 July 1670); Livro 41, f. 233v. (30 October 1672).

27. Also important in these campaigns was another officer later to become important in the history of Brazil, Gomes Freire de Andrade. He served as governor of Maranhão (1684-88). See Ericeira, *História*, 4:326-27.

28. ANTT, Chancelaria Afonso VI, Doações, Livro 41, f. 12.

29. [Alexandre de Paixão], *Monstruosidades do tempo e da fortuna*, edited by Damião Peres, 4 vols. in one (Oporto, 1938-39), 2:113-14.

30. Rocha Pitta said of him: "foi mais alentado que venturoso." See Sebastião da Rocha Pitta, *História da América Portugueza (1724)*, 2d ed. (Lisbon, 1880), p. 198.

31. Gastão Melo de Matos, "Panfletos do seculo xvii," *Anais. Academia Portuguesa da História. Ciclo da Restauração de Portugal* 10 (1946): 64, 146-49. The article discusses a satirical list of plays in which the playwrights are political figures who best fit the titles given the plays. "No intente el que no es dichoso" is actually the title of a play attributed to Rojas Zorilla.

32. *Ibid.*

33. Rocha Pitta, *História*, p. 198.

34. ANTT, Chancelaria Ordem de Cristo, Livro 38, f. 422-422v; Livro 35, f. 75. He also held the commandery of São Romão da Fonte Cuberta of the Order of Aviz, apparently acquired from his father-in-law. The office of constable major of Covilhã was inherited from his father and maternal grandfather.

35. For example, ANTT, Chancelaria Afonso VI, Doações, Livro 38, f. 233; Livro 18, f. 133-133v.; Livro 50, f. 107v.; Livro 13, f. 316.

36. ANTT, Chancelaria Afonso VI, Doações, Livro 41, f. 190-190v. He received the right to pass the title to his eldest son, 10 January 1672. See ANTT, Chancelaria Afonso VI, Doações, Livro 41, f. 163v.

37. Felgueiras Gayo, *Nobilario de familias de Portugal*, 28 vols. (Braga, 1940), 20: 18n.

38. *Consulta* Conselho Ultramarino, AHU, Bahia *papéis avulsos*, caixa 11, 2d series uncataloged (25 September 1675).

39. ANTT, Chancelaria Afonso VI, Doações, Livro 41, f. 163v.

40. *Consulta* Conselho Ultramarino, AHU, Bahia *papéis avulsos*, caixa 12, 1st series uncataloged (25 May 1676).

41. Ross Bardwell, "The Governors of Portugal's South Atlantic Empire in the Seventeenth Century" (Ph.D. dissertation, University of California, Santa Barbara, 1974).

42. *DHBNR*, 10 (1929):5-7; 5 (1928):176-77.

43. Letter to Pedro de Almeida, governor of Pernambuco (23 February 1675), *DHBNR*, 10 (1929):134-37.

44. Letter to Câmara of Porto Seguro (28 May 1671), *DHBNR*, 6 (1928):171-72; letter to Capitão Mór of Itamaraca, *DHBNR*, 10 (1929):37-39.

45. Letter to governor of Pernambuco (28 May 1672), *DHBNR*, 10 (1929):57.

46. Letter to governor of Rio de Janeiro (20 February 1672), *DHBNR*, 6 (1928): 272-73.

47. Regimento de governador . . . Afonso Furtado de Mendonça, Arquivo da Casa de Cadaval, n. 300, par. 5.

190 NOTES TO THE INTRODUCTION

48. *Consulta*, Overseas Council (2 December 1679), AHU, Codice 252, f. 57-57v.
49. Letter to Dom Pedro de Almeida (23 February 1675), *DHBNR*, 10 (1929):134-37.
50. *Ibid*. Afonso Furtado was, at the time, not convinced that the Paulistas would have the same success against escaped slaves as against Indians. The maroon community of Palmares had existed in the area of Alagoas from the beginning of the seventeenth century. It was finally destroyed in 1694. See Edson Carneiro, *O quilombo dos Palmares*, 3d ed. (Rio de Janeiro, 1966).
51. AHU, Bahia *papéis avulsos*, caixa 11 (24 May 1673), 1st series uncataloged.
52. Carlos Alberto Ferreira, *Inventário dos manuscritos da Biblioteca da Ajuda referentes à América do Sul* (Coimbra, 1946), p. 372.
53. Antônio Marques de Perada, "Bahia restaurada pello felis governo de excellentisimo Senhor Marques das Minas," Biblioteca Nacional de Lisboa, Secção de Reservados, Fundo geral, codice 300-301. Marquês de Perada had resided in Bahia. See ASCMB, C/1/307, f. 5v.
54. For published examples of this genre, see Julio de Mello de Castro, *Historia panegyrica da vida de Dinis de Mello de Castro, primeiro Conde de Galveas* (Lisbon, 1752); Eusebio de Matos, *Oração funebre do illmo. e revmo. Sr. D. Estevam dos Sanctos Bisbo do Brasil, celebradas a 14 de Julho de 1672* (Lisbon, 1735).
55. Cf. Eduardo Camacho Guizado, *La elegía funeral en la poesía española* (Madrid, 1969), p. 158. Eulogistic biographies of viceroys of India were apparently not uncommon. Cf. José Freire de Monterroyo Mascarenhas, *Epanaphora Indica*, 5 parts (Lisbon, 1746-50), concerning the administration of the Marquis of Castelo Novo as viceroy of India.
56. *DHBNR*, 87 (1950):225-26; AHU Bahia *papéis avulsos*, caixa 12, 1st series uncataloged (8 August 1675); Arquivo da Câmara Municipal de Salvador, Livro 159, f. 161; ANRJ, Codice 540, assento 56. See also Stuart B. Schwartz, *Sovereignty and Society in Colonial Brazil* (Berkeley, 1973).
57. AHU, Bahia *papéis avulsos*, caixa 12, 1st series uncataloged; AHU, Codice 252, f. 19v.-20 (18 June 1673).
58. There is a considerable literature on Fernão Dias Pais and his expedition. For an adequate summary see Pedro Calmon, *História do Brasil*, 3:775-81.
59. Cf. Affonso Ávila, *O lúdico e as projeções do mundo barroco* (São Paulo, 1971); also his *Resíduos seiscentistas em Minas* (Belo Horizonte, 1967).
60. Wilson Martins, *História da inteligência brasileira*, 3 vols. (São Paulo, 1977-78), 1:206-25. See also the journal *Universitas* 2 (January-April 1969), devoted entirely to the theme of baroque culture in Brazil.
61. Cf. Adrian Fortescue, *The Ceremonies of the Roman Rite Described* (London, 1940). See also Ralph E. Giesey, *The Royal Funeral Ceremony in Renaissance France* (Geneva, 1960); Erwin Panofsky, *Tomb Sculpture* (New York, 1964). On changing concepts of death see Michael Vovelle, *Pieté Baroque et Dechristianisation: les attitudes devant le mort en Provence au xviiie siècle* (Paris, 1973), and Phillipe Ariès, *Western Attitudes toward Death: From the Middle Ages to the Present*, translated from French by Patricia Ranum (Baltimore, 1978).

62. On European thought and religion in this period see Henri Busson, *La religion des classiques (1660-1685)* (Paris, 1948). See also Paul Hazard, *The European Mind, 1680-1715* (Cleveland, 1963). An excellent introduction to the art and aesthetics of the period is Germain Bazin, *The Baroque* (London, 1968).

63. The bibliography on Vieira and Matos is extensive. Martins, *História da inteligência brasileira*, 1:180-238, presents a penetrating analysis of these men and their milieu as well as noting the relevant bibliography.

64. Pedro Calmon, *História da literatura bahiana* (Rio de Janeiro, 1949), pp. 25-34. Botelho de Oliveira dedicated two poems to Afonso Furtado in his *Musica de Parnaso* (Lisbon, 1705).

65. José de Wanderley Pinho, *História de um engenho do Recôncavo* (Rio de Janeiro, 1946), p. 151; *DHBNR*, 3 (1928):320-21; *Documentos históricos do Arquivo Municipal. Atas da Câmara*, 6 vols. (1944-49), 3:311-13. Unfortunately, the council's letter says nothing about the petitioner and deals only with his invention.

66. Aside from Schwartz, *Sovereignty and Society*, and A. J. R. Russell-Wood, *Fidalgos and Philanthropists. The Santa Casa da Misericórdia da Bahia, 1550-1755* (Berkeley, 1968), there have been three recent American doctoral theses that have studied the social fabric of seventeenth-century Bahia in detail, making intensive use of local notary records. None of these works has revealed anything about Juan Lopes Sierra. The matter is complicated, however, by the fact that the notary records of Salvador are available only for the period after 1684, a date most likely subsequent to Juan Lopes Sierra's death. See: Rae Flory, "Bahian Society in the Mid-Colonial Period: The Sugar Planters, Tobacco Growers, Merchants, and Artisans of Salvador and the Recôncavo, 1680-1725" (Ph.D. thesis, University of Texas, 1978); Susan Soeiro, "A Baroque Nunnery: The Economic and Social Role of a Colonial Convent: Santa Clara do Destêrro, Salvador, Bahia, 1677-1800" (Ph.D. thesis, New York University, 1974); David G. Smith, "The Mercantile Class of Portugal and Brazil in the Seventeenth Century: A Socio-Economic Study of the Merchants of Lisbon and Bahia, 1620-1690" (Ph.D. thesis, University of Texas, 1975).

NOTES TO THE TRANSLATION

1. "Humble gift" in the original is *corcho de agua*. The reference is obscure. The story does not appear in either Plutarch or Herodotus.

2. At this point the following passage appears in the Ajuda manuscript: "y no puedo appreender ni allo quien escrivia un cuarderno por media pataca quieren ocho reales por esso nova perfeecto cree desto mio lo que qui sierves de lo Nuestro Heroe todo y creme que dixe mucho por desir desseoso de que llevase El Navio este f^a."

Between folios 6 and 7 of the Ajuda manuscript is the following poem.

192 NOTES TO THE TRANSLATION

A Morte do Senhor Afonso Furtado Castro Rios de Mendonça
Acrostico em Eccos
Soneto

Affonso a quem neste prestado	—estado
Finalizou a tão devida	—vida
Fes alentado em tão sentida	—ida
O golpe atros de dezamado	—amado
Nunca sevio a mal soldado	—dado
Sempre a bondade consentida	—tida
O ceu ter a alma desunida	—unida
Fes a alma o corpo dezatado	—atado
Vencerão sempre seus sombrios	—brios
Ralhos sem ter de girigonça	—onça
Tanto vencendo de Alemcastro	—Castro
Abrio de Sangue aos Hiberios	—rios
Destro nas armas or Mendonça	—onça
Oje nos ceos pello de Castro	—astro
Sera prenda de Rodrigo	

Two other acrostic poems from the Ajuda manuscript appear on pages 203-5 of this volume.

3. Sebola is actually Caius Mucius Scaevola, whose opposition dissuaded the Etruscan Lars Porsenna from his attempt to capture Rome and establish a tyranny in 508 B.C. The incident is taken from Livy ii-12-13. On this episode see Robert M. Ogilvie, *A Commentary on Livy, Books 1-5* (Oxford, 1965), pp. 262-66.

4. Viriathus, a Lusitanian, led a series of guerrilla campaigns against the Romans in Hispania (Iberia). He forced Rome to terms but was betrayed and assassinated in 139 B.C. He has become a symbol of Spanish nationality. The reference to the two Alexanders is probably to Alexander Severus (Marcus Aurelius) and Alexander III of Macedonia called "The Great."

5. The Argives Cleobis and Biton died in the temple of Hera in a story related by Herodotus (I, 31). The people of Argos erected statues to them at Delphi.

6. Alexandre de Sousa Freire had served as governor of the fortress of Mazagão in North Africa before he took control of the government at Bahia 16 June 1667. Although he was ill during much of his administration, his major efforts were directed toward a campaign against the Indians of the sertão of Bahia and the suppression of a civil rebellion in Sergipe de El-Rey.

7. Three aspects of this paragraph deserve notice or explanation. The peace between Spain and Portugal that formally recognized Portuguese independence and the end of the war that had begun with the revolt of Portugal from Hapsburg control in 1640 was signed 13 February 1668 through English mediation. Note here and throughout the manuscript the use of "His Highness" rather than the usual "His Majesty" in reference to the ruler. Forms of address were carefully regulated and jealously guarded in Europe during this period, and Portugal was no exception. The basic rules were set forth by a royal order of 1597. The reason for the less-elevated form, "His Highness" (*Sua Alteza*),

is easily explained by the political situation that existed in Portugal in 1676, the date of authorship. King Afonso VI, who had assumed the throne in 1656, was a sickly and profligate man, much under the influence of his French wife and his chief councillor, the Count of Castel Melhor. Court intrigue, failure to produce an heir, and diplomatic pressures eventually brought about a palace coup that placed Afonso's brother Pedro in power as prince regent in 1668 with the approval of the *cortes*, or estates general. He ruled as regent from 1668 to 1683 and then as king (Dom Pedro II) from 1683 to 1706. During the period covered by the work presented here (1668-75), Afonso remained a virtual captive while his brother Pedro ruled as regent and was, therefore, entitled to "Highness" but not "Majesty," which was reserved for the monarch. See Luís F. L. Cintra, *Sobre "Formas de Tratamento" na lingua portuguesa* (Lisbon, 1972).

Finally, this passage provides a clear indication that the James Ford Bell Library copy is the original, written in Bahia, and that the manuscript of the Biblioteca da Ajuda is a presentation copy, written in Portugal. The Bell Library manuscript reads: "el tratado de la paz entre *aquella* [italics added] y la española corona." The Ajuda manuscript varies by saying: "*esta* [italics added] y la española corona."

8. Governor general of India Antônio de Melo e Castro (1662-66).

9. "Southern towns" is *vilas do baixo*. The captaincy of Bahia was divided into administrative units, or *comarcas*. The *sertão do baixo* comprised the area south of the Bay of All Saints.

10. This is Manoel Barbosa de Mesquita. The incident is recounted with some detail in Rocha Pitta. Barbosa de Mesquita had come from Lisbon in 1670 to exercise the post of captain in Cairú. During a festival day when all the townsfolk were in the principal church, an Indian attack caught them by surprise. Barbosa de Mesquita and his men sallied forth from the church. His valorous action probably saved the town, but he died from his wounds before the Indians withdrew (pp. 192-93). The attack was probably carried out by the Aimorés, a powerful group that resisted the Portuguese in this region for over two centuries.

11. Don Francisco de Távora was probably the brother-in-law of Afonso Furtado de Castro do Rio de Mendonça. The attack of the Duke of Sonho refers to "Duke of Sueño" in the original. This is actually the Count of Sonho (Soyo), a major and powerful vassal of the Manicongo (King of the Congo). Governor Francisco de Távora had initiated a campaign against him in 1670. For these events see Antônio de Olivera de Cadornega, *História geral das guerras angolanas*, 1680, 3 vols. (Lisbon, 1972), 2:259-359; 3:194.

12. Montserrate is a Benedictine monastery located outside the city of Barcelona, and Our Lady of Montserrate is the patron saint of Catalonia. In the seventeenth century the Portuguese poet and author Francisco Manuel de Mello referred to Salvador as the "Antarctic Montserrate." The Benedictine monastery is on a height overlooking Barcelona just as the city of Salvador is situated on a high escarpment. This physical similarity probably caused the comparison. Legend has it that the actual builder of the chapel in Bahia was a Spanish soldier who was particularly devoted to Our Lady of Montserrate. See José Carlos Ferreira, *Memoria sobre o Estado da Bahia* (Bahia, 1893), p. 311. See also note 49 below.

13. The author is mistaken about the name. This is not Antônio but Francisco Telles de Meneses, a wealthy Bahian who had purchased the office of chief constable (*alcaide-*

mor) in 1667. He was the stepson of the High Court judge Cristóvão de Burgos and was known for his quick tongue and high-handed ways. He became the center of a series of family feuds in 1682 involving the principal figures of Bahia; these feuds led to swordplay in the streets and to his assassination in 1683. See Schwartz, *Sovereignty and Society in Colonial Brazil*, pp. 275-79.

14. The municipal council of São Cristóvão, capital of Sergipe de El-Rey, had complained against taxes levied on the captaincy and about the abuse of authority by Jorge Rabello Leite, the governor. The city had risen up against him. Afonso Furtado arrested the leaders of the revolt, issued a general pardon, and replaced the abusive official with a new governor, João Munhos. The relevant documents are printed in Felisbello Firmo de Oliveira Freire, *História de Sergipe (1575-1855)* (Rio de Janeiro, 1891), pp. 159-63.

15. Mentioned here are two of the wealthiest men in Brazil during this period, João Peixoto Viegas and Antônio Guedes de Brito. See Appendix A for biographical information. Paiäiäs, an Indian group of the interior, are referred to as Payases throughout the manuscript.

16. On João Matos de Aguiar see Appendix A. The Order of Christ was created in 1369 as a successor to the Order of Templars and was the most important and prestigious religious-military order of knighthood in the Portuguese empire. Although its military functions had all but disappeared by the sixteenth century, its habit and pensions were still coveted. The Orders of Santiago and Aviz were the other Portuguese knightly orders of the period.

17. These details of the contract with Estevão Ribeiro Baião Parente can be found in no other source. The most complete description of these activities appears in Afonso de Escragnolle Taunay, *HGBP*, 5:2-47. Various patents of appointment of the Paulista leaders can be found in *DHBNR*, 24:262-72.

18. The manuscript is in error and refers to Olivelas rather than Odivelas. The incident at Odivelas took place May 10, 1671, when a young man named Antônio Ferreira Soares broke into the church of this small town near Lisbon and stole a few items from the altar. The incident was minor but the impact great. Penitential processions were organized throughout Portugal, and the desecration was used as an excuse to increase persecution of "New Christians" (descendants of Jews). At the time, feelings ran high against New Christians because of their importance in Portugal's economic life. When Ferreira was captured and it was discovered that he, in fact, did have New Christian parents, the crown issued a series of edicts further limiting the roles of New Christians in public life and expelling some from the kingdom. New Christians argued that Ferreira was nothing more than a common thief and that the incident had been staged to increase popular hatred toward them. The incident's widespread impact is documented here by the reaction of Afonso Furtado and the measures taken. For a contemporary view see [Alexandre de Paixão], *Monstruosidades do tempo e da fortuna (1662-1680)*, edited by Damião Peres, 4 vols. (Oporto, 1938-39), 2:120-25; 3:10-19. The incident is detailed in Carl Hanson, "Economy and Society in Baroque Portugal, 1668-1703" (Ph.D. thesis, University of New Mexico, 1978), pp. 30-38. The editor would like to thank Mr. Hanson for providing copies of the relevant materials.

19. The "two senates" (*los dos cabildos*) refers to the *cabido*, or ecclesiastical council, of the cathedral and to the *senado da Câmara*, or town council.

20. The Royal Tribunal of Justice refers to the *Relação*, or High Court of Appeals. See Schwartz, *Sovereignty and Society in Colonial Brazil* (Berkeley, 1973), which discusses this tribunal, its functions and personnel.

21. Inácio Faia was born in 1630 in Lisbon and entered the Society of Jesus at the age of seventeen. He served in Recife, Rio de Janeiro, and Bahia and was a preacher of great reputation. Here the author is probably mistaken that Faia was father superior of the order, since our principal authority, Serafim Leite (*HCJB*, 10:214), does not list him as such.

22. Francisco de Matos, a noted Jesuit teacher, author, preacher, and administrator. Born in 1636 in Lisbon, he came to Brazil at age sixteen and professed in the Jesuit Order in 1670. He returned to Portugal in 1674 and remained there for eighteen years as Procurator General. He returned to Brazil, where he became Provincial in 1697.

23. The editor could not identify the specific event, although the charge against the Protestant rebels in the Low Countries seems to be formulaic.

24. Philip IV died in 1621, not 1622. Note that Lopes Sierra refers to the Hapsburg monarchs of Spain and Portugal by their Spanish numbering. Philip IV of Spain was actually Philip III of Portugal. The incident described here took place in Granada July 25, 1621. The reference to a "poet of Granada" may be the author's citation of his own earlier work and a revelation, therefore, of his place of birth. See Angel González Palencia, ed., *Notícias de Madrid, 1621-1627* (Madrid, 1942), p. 7.

25. The instruction, or *regimento*, issued to Afonso Furtado de Mendonça is preserved in the private archive of the dukes of Cadaval (Codice 1027f [KVI If., L. 342v-363]) from which an extract has been printed in Virginia Rau and Maria Fernanda Gomes da Silva, eds., *Os manuscritos de Arquivo da Casa de Cadaval respeitantes ao Brasil*, 2 vols. (Coimbra, 1956), 1:211-29. This set of instructions makes only passing reference to the two matters, mines and Indians, noted here. However, an abbreviated set of instructions consisting of twelve articles does ask for an inquiry about saltpeter mines. The silver and amethysts appear to be a colorful addition of Lopes Sierra based on the governor's own later initiatives. Cf. AHU, Bahia, *papéis avulsos*, caixa 11 (28 September 1674).

26. Despite the description of difficulties, there may have been more to the *São Pedro de Rates*'s call at Salvador than is at first apparent. Many of the great ships in the India run made a habit of calling at Bahia for trade as well as "repairs." Royal instructions to Afonso Furtado, in fact, had specifically warned against this illicit commerce (par. 33 of the Cadaval ms.). The *São Pedro de Rates* called at Salvador not only in 1672, but again in 1673 on the way to India and in 1676 on a return voyage to Portugal. See José Roberto de Amaral Lapa, *A Bahia e a Carreira da India* (São Paulo, 1968), pp. 334-36.

27. Pedro Gomes was another wealthy Bahian. See Appendix A.

28. This sonnet does not appear in the Ajuda manuscript.

29. Afonso Furtado de Castro do Rio de Mendonça was admitted to the Holy House of Mercy as a brother of superior standing on 3 July 1671, and he exercised the chief office of *Provedor* in that organization the same year. The *Santa Casa da Misericórdia* was a prestigious lay brotherhood devoted primarily to charitable activities. Membership as a brother of superior standing was socially desirable, and the most powerful planters, merchants, and bureaucrats were found on its rolls. See A. J. R. Russell-Wood, *Fidalgos and Philanthropists. The Santa Casa da Misericórdia da Bahia, 1550-1755* (Berkeley, 1968).

A useful listing of the membership in the seventeenth century is Neusa Rodrigues Esteves, *Catalogo dos irmãos da Santa Casa da Misericórdia da Bahia* (Salvador, 1977).

30. For a short biography of Francisco Fernandes do Sim, or "da Ilha" as he was called, see Appendix A.

31. Legal opposition to Francisco Fernandes do Sim's endowment of the Misericórdia raised by his son-in-law, Nicolão Aranha, is not mentioned in Russell-Wood's study of that institution (*Fidalgos and Philanthropists*) and was apparently unknown to him.

32. The See of Salvador had remained vacant for as long as the War of Restoration (1640-68) had continued between Portugal and Spain. During this period Spanish influence in Rome prevented the filling of benefices in the "rebellious" Portuguese territories. Father Estevão dos Santos, who had formerly administered the church of São Vicente de Fora in Lisbon, was the first to occupy the Bahian See after peace was declared. He died within three months of his arrival and was buried in the Cathedral of Salvador. See José Antônio Caldas, *Noticia geral desta capitania da Bahia* (1759), facsimile edition (Bahia, 1951), p. 36. See also Father Eusebio de Mattos, *Oração funebre nas Exequias do . . . D. Estevam dos Santos Bispo do Brasil* (Lisbon, 1735).

33. The passage is unclear. Apparently Dona Francisca de Sande had received a loan and would be excused from the interest payments in return for surrender of her claim. Still, in 1694 Dona Francisca de Sande was listed by the Misericórdia as owing over 275 *milréis* of interest on a loan of 1,600 *milréis*. "Lista de pessoas que devem a esta Santa Casa de Mïa. dineiro a rezão de juro . . ." (AHU, Bahia, *papéis avulsos*, caixa 17).

34. Bento Suriel (Camiglio), long thought to be Italian, is described here as a Frenchman, for the first time. He arrived in Bahia by way of Pernambuco and in 1672 received a commission to explore for saltpeter mines along the São Francisco River. In 1673 he was named an assistant in the patent given to Don Rodrigo de Castelo Branco. The two men argued, and Bento Suriel was imprisoned for a short period. Released by order of Governor Afonso Furtado, he continued a career of mining exploration in the São Francisco River valley during the 1680s. He became friendly with Domingos Jorge Velho and those Paulistas engaged in the campaign to destroy the great maroon community at Palmares. Sometime after 1694 he returned to Portugal to plead before the crown the case of these Paulistas for rewards. See Carvalho Franco, *Dicionário de bandeirantes e sertanistas do Brasil* (São Paulo, 1953), pp. 96-97; *DHBNR*, 25:260-63.

35. This most likely refers to the senior councilman (*vereador*) of the Câmara of Salvador.

36. In the marriage arrangements between Charles II of England and Catherine of Bragança, daughter of João IV, concluded by treaty on 23 June 1661, Portugal agreed to cede the cities of Tangier and Bombay to England and to pay a sum of two million *cruzados*. This money, the *dote da inglaterra*, combined with an indemnity paid to the Dutch, was raised by levies on the municipal councils throughout the Portuguese empire. Collection was continually in arrears and was the cause of much grumbling in Brazil.

37. An earlier junta had been formed by Governor Alexandre de Sousa Freire in 1670 to raise money to pay for the Paulista expedition against the Indians of Bahia. João de Matos de Aguiar had served as the treasurer of the funds collected. See *Atas da Câmara*, 5:42-43.

38. Bernardo Vieira Ravasco was the brother of the famous Jesuit Antônio Vieira. See Appendix A for a brief biography.

39. The Portuguese classified the Brazilian Indians into two principal categories: those who spoke languages of the Tupí-Guaraní family and those who spoke languages unrelated to Tupí. Since Tupí-Guaraní speakers occupied most of the coastline in the sixteenth century, the Portuguese, and especially the Jesuits, learned to communicate in these languages, which under the Jesuits were simplified into a Tupí-based dialect called by the Portuguese *brasilico* (Brazilian) or *lingua geral* (the general language). Indians of other linguistic groups were commonly referred to as *Tapuyas* or speakers of *lingua travada* (twisted tongue), that is, languages unintelligible to Tupí speakers (these would include Gê, Carajá, Carib, Arawak, etc.). Because the Tupí-Guaraní speakers tended to practice agriculture and the Tapuyas did not, cultural evaluations were associated with these terms. Important studies of the variations of Tupí and the development of the *lingua geral* have been made by the Bahian scholar Federico G. Edelweiss. See, for example, *Estudos Tupis e Tupi-guaranis* (Rio de Janeiro, 1969).

40. The manuscript calls the latter two tribes the "Payahazes and the Supoceayas." The first group is undoubtedly the Paiäiäs and the second probably the Sapoiás. Both groups of *Tapuyas* of the Bahian interior were first described in 1656 by a Jesuit missionary, Father Antônio Pinto. They inhabited the area near the present-day city of Jacobina. The Paiäiäs had probably been driven westward by European pressure since Father Pinto found that they already viewed the Portuguese as enemies at the time of his arrival among them. Military expeditions were directed against them in 1658 and again in 1669 while the Jesuits worked to establish a village of Paiäiäs under their direction. João Peixoto Viegas, the major landowner in this region, wished to use the Paiäiäs for his own purposes. A conflict over their control developed between him and the Jesuits that was not resolved until 1680, in favor of the Fathers. In 1758 a listing of Indian villages in Bahia reported only one small remnant of Paiäiäs. See Serafim Leite, *História da Companhia de Jesus no Brasil*, 10 vols. (Lisbon, 1938-50) 5:270-80; *DHBNR*, 25: 397-404.

41. *Palo blando* (soft wood) is most likely the *pau-mole*, but could be any one of a number of plants characteristic of the sertão. Among the types of vegetation locally called *caatinga* or *mata seca* are a large variety of xerophytic plants with small leaves and large roots capable of storing water, especially well adapted to arid conditions.

42. Caravatá is the generic term for a large number of bromeliad species. All major naturalists of colonial Brazil include some reference to these plants. The broad leaves in some species were used to prepare poisons for fishing. For an illustration see (Frei) Cristováó de Lisboa, *História dos animais e ávores do Maranhão*, edited by Jaime Walter (Lisbon, 1967), p. 120, f. 144.

43. Otinga is the present-day town of Utinga on the Rio Utinga. The word *u-tinga* is a corruption of the Tupí *y-tinga*, or clear water.

44. The Treaty of Tordesillas, signed between Spain and Portugal in 1494, had established a boundary between the possessions of the two empires in the New World. During the seventeenth century, Portuguese backwoodsmen searching for Indian captives and mineral wealth had pushed well beyond the unmarked frontier into the Spanish Indies. Establishment of recognized boundaries between Brazil and the Spanish empire, especially in the Rio de la Plata and the Amazon regions, was the cause of both renegotiation and conflict throughout the eighteenth century.

45. Taunay, *HGBP*, 5:34, states that the triumph took place in February 1673 rather

than the date given here of August 1672. Taunay also claimed that 750 captives were brought into the city and that an equal number had died in the march to Salvador from a "near plague." The year 1673 was also one of drought and shortage of food.

46. The word *panacu* is Tupí for basket.

47. For a brief biography of Castelo Branco, see Appendix A.

48. The term "noble of the King's household" (*fidalgo da casa*) refers to one of the ranks of nobility. A distinction was drawn between those who were noble by birth (*moço fidalgo*) and those who received the honor in return for service to the crown. The distinction is well expressed in the following explanation of the late seventeenth century made by an English observer: "There is none can be *moço fidalgo* but he whose ancestors were *fidalgos*, therefore on occasion they are called *moços fidalgos* even when they are *fidalgos*, because it supposes them to be of noble descent, *de sangue illustre* [illustrious blood] they call it here, whereas there be many *fidalgos* who are either themselves made so by the King for some good service or that are but immediate descendants of such, who are only of no ignoble blood *de sangue limpio* [clean blood] . . . and these are called *fidalgos da casa del rey*, that have no other *fidalguia* then what the King's book gives them; and they are very much disregarded by the others; in so much that the . . . *fidalgos* will never marry into their families though they be ever so rich." From PRO, SP 9/207, n. 24, f. 592.

49. From the day of his arrival in Brazil until his death Afonso Furtado maintained his particular devotion for Our Lady of Montserrate, the patron saint of Catalonia, favoring her church over the larger and more magnificent temples of the city. Governor Francisco de Sousa (1591-1602) had constructed a small fort and a chapel of Montserrate and had later donated the church to the Benedictines of Salvador. The little church, built on a small peninsula and surrounded on three sides by the sea, became a place of pilgrimage for the inhabitants of the Recôncavo. Brazilian historian Pedro Calmon suggests that Afonso Furtado's particular devotion to this church as well as his abiding interest in mines were transmitted to him by his wife's relative, the former governor, Francisco de Sousa. See Pedro Calmon, *História do Brasil*, 5 vols. (Rio de Janeiro, 1959) 3:746n.; Prefeitura de Salvador, *Mont-Serrat o Forte e a igreja* (Pequeno guia das igrejas da Bahia) (Salvador, 1966). See also Francisco Adolfo de Varnhagen, *História geral do Brasil*, 7th ed., 6 vols. (São Paulo, 1962), 2:52.

50. The Third Order of St. Francis was the most prestigious lay brotherhood in Bahia, with the exception of the Misericórdia. Membership was limited to the social elite of the colony, and the order carefully excluded anyone with mechanic or artisan origins and those "tainted" with mulatto or "New Christian" (Jewish) origins. The chapel of the Third Order of St. Francis remains today one of the most beautiful churches in Salvador. See Marieta Alves, *História da Venerável Ordem Terceira da Penetência do Seráfico P^e São Francisco da Congregação da Bahia* (Bahia, 1948).

51. Note here that the Paulistas sent these Indians to São Paulo rather than selling them in Bahia. This situation indicates the limited demand for Indian laborers on the plantations of the Northeast.

52. This passage is clarified by the patent granted to Manuel de Inojosa as Captain of the town of Santo Antônio da Conquista, which had been established "in the lands where they had conquered and destroyed the nation and village of the Cochos." Inojo-

sa was chosen because of his experience in that region. Patent of (?) October 1673, printed in Accioli, *MHPB*, 2:233-34.

53. See pages 86-87, 90-92.

54. The great silver mine at Potosí (in present-day Bolivia) had been opened by the Spanish in 1545. Through most of the sixteenth and seventeenth centuries it was the richest mine in the Spanish empire and became a symbol of the wealth of the Indies. The Portuguese believed that similar mines must exist in Brazil. Failing to discover such mines, the Portuguese in Brazil were not averse to deriving some profit from Potosí itself. Between 1580 and 1622 an active trade developed with Potosí by way of Buenos Aires and the Rio de la Plata. After 1622, when an inland customs house to control this commerce was established at Córdoba, the Portuguese turned increasingly to smuggling. Through much of the seventeenth century, Peruvian silver coins were the common currency in Brazil. See the classic study by Alice Canabrava, *O comércio português no Rio da Prata, 1580-1640* (São Paulo, 1944).

55. "Turks" in this context undoubtedly refers to Moroccan or Algerine corsairs. This is supported by a letter of the famous Jesuit Padre Antônio Vieira, who mentioned the shipwreck and the loss of the mineral samples. See Vieira to Duarte Ribeiro de Macedo (Rome, 14 November 1674), in João Lucio de Azevedo, ed., *Cartas do Padre Antônio Vieira*, 3 vols. (Lisbon, 1971), 3:122-24. On the Barbary corsairs in this period see G. N. Clark, "The Barbary Corsairs in the Seventeenth Century," *Cambridge Historical Journal*, 8 (1945-46): 22-35, and Godfrey Fisher, *Barbary Legend, War, Trade and Piracy in North Africa, 1415-1830* (Oxford, 1953).

56. Afonso Furtado and Dona Maria de Távora had three children. The elder son, Jorge Furtado de Mendonça, inherited the title of Viscount of Barbacena. A daughter, Dona Magdalena de Távora never married. The third child was João Furtado de Mendonça. His secondary status and the realization of it probably prompted him to accompany his father to Brazil and to seek his fortune there. In 1670, on the eve of his departure for Brazil, he petitioned for and received an annual stipend of 200 *milréis* that he planned to use in a bid for the whaling contract in Bahia (AHU, Bahia, *papéis avulsos*, caixa 11). Having his father as governor did not retard João Furtado's progress in the world. Upon arrival in Brazil Afonso Furtado removed an elderly veteran, Álvaro de Azevedo, from his post as field master and gave the position to his son, João. Complaint from the aggrieved party led to his reinstatement, but João Furtado was not removed from office (AHU, Bahia, *papéis avulsos*, caixa 11, 1st ser., uncataloged). He and his cousin Antônio de Sousa e Meneses both received land grants from Afonso Furtado. These were later the cause of a major lawsuit between the heirs of Afonso Furtado and Field Master Pedro Gomes (ANTT, Coleção São Vicente livro 13, f. 264, dated 12 October 1676). In 1685 João Furtado de Mendonça was appointed governor of Rio de Janeiro, where he served with distinction, according to Balthazar da Silva Lisboa, *Annaes do Rio de Janeiro*, 7 vols. (Rio de Janeiro, 1834-35), 5:26-28.

57. The reference here probably refers to the Companhia Geral de Comércio do Brasil (General Company of Commerce of Brazil) established in 1649 to stimulate Brazilian economic development. The company sent two fleets a year to Brazil. As a monopoly company it maintained control over the sale of wine, olive oil, codfish, and manioc flour. Conflict with local interests eventually led to a royal attempt to restructure the company

in 1662, and in the following year it was transformed into a government board, the Junta de Comércio. Until it was abolished in 1720, this board administered the movement of the fleets to Brazil. A good short essay on the Portuguese commercial companies is provided by Jorge Borges de Macedo in the *DHP*, 1:636-44.

58. This reference and the following description of the expedition of Manuel de Inojosa to the Rio Quitose, headwaters of the Rio das Contas, appear to be the first mention of this *bandeira*. The account is probably based on the report prepared by the scribe Antônio Rodrigues Botão. Traditional historiography of the *bandeirantes* makes no mention of this expedition. Taunay's *HGBP* contains no reference to it.

59. Plutarch, *Life of Alexander*, 77.

60. Taxes in Brazil were farmed to private individuals who bid for the three-year contract and who hoped to make a profit on the difference between their bid and the amount collected.

61. Agostinho de Figueiredo had served as captain major and governor of São Vicente since 1665. In 1673 he received a commission as administrator of the southern mines. He took up residence in Curitiba, Paraná, in the supposed area of the mines. See Carvalho Franco, *DBSB*, p. 161.

62. Francisco Manuel de Mello (1608-66) was an outstanding figure of Portuguese letters in the seventeenth century. His works in poetry, history, social criticism, and politics were widely read and admired. Educated in Portugal, he served in a number of campaigns on both land and sea, some of which became the subjects of his pen. In Spain when the Portuguese restoration of 1640 began, he was arrested in Madrid as a suspected rebel, but he eventually gained freedom and joined the forces supporting João, duke of Bragança, the Portuguese pretender who became Dom João IV. He led an embassy to England, but in 1644 he was arrested as an accomplice in the murder of a member of the count of Vila Nova's household. It has been suggested that the real reason for this arrest was his competition with the duke of Bragança for the favors of the countess of Vila Nova. In any case, he was exiled to Brazil in 1655 and remained there until 1658 when, after Dom João IV's death, Mello was pardoned. He returned to Portugal, where he served the court in several diplomatic posts. The classic biography of his life is Edgar Prestage, *D. Francisco Manuel de Mello, esboço biographico* (Coimbra, 1914); for a short biographical sketch see *DHP*, 3:12-13.

63. Afonso Furtado's illness continued for over two years before his death. His own comment on the final attack that resulted in his death was, "I have been bled five times for an *ersipela* that attacked me while at Mont-Serrate and which did not allow me to finish a novena; but I am now much improved." He wrote this to the governor of Pernambuco, Dom Pedro de Almeida, 1 November 1675 and he died 26 November. *DHBNR*, 10 (1929): 130, 158-59, 181.

64. Erysipelas, sometimes called St. Anthony's fire, is an acute febrile disease often resulting in inflammation of the skin and subcutaneous tissues.

65. "Tibe soli pecavi" is from Psalms 50:6 and is a part of the burial service. See *Exsequiale pro adultis et parvulis* (New York, 1957), p. 6.

66. Alexandre de Gusmão was born in Lisbon in 1629. At age fifteen, in 1644, he accompanied his family to Brazil. After studying at the Jesuit College in Rio de Janeiro he professed in the Order in 1664. An educator of note, he served as rector of the Jesuit College at Bahia. He is particularly remembered as the author of a number of works on

moral and religious themes including what is considered by many to be the precursor of the Brazilian novel, a work entitled *História do predestinado peregrino*, published in Lisbon in 1682. Father Gusmão died in Bahia in 1724.

67. Antônio de Sousa e Meneses, who had accompanied his uncle to Brazil and to whom Lopes Sierra dedicated this work. He had been made captain of an infantry *terço* (regiment) of João Furtado de Medonça, his cousin, by a patent of 14 May 1671. See *DHBNR*, 24 (1934):158-60.

68. Afonso Furtado was the first governor general to die in Brazil, and apparently due to oversight no formal means of succession had been established. The fact that Afonso Furtado rose from his deathbed to settle this problem speaks to his devotion to duty, but there may have been other reasons that impelled him. The men selected as members of the interim triumvirate were important members of Bahian society. Two, Álvaro de Azevedo, a veteran of campaigns in Europe and the senior field master, and Antônio Guedes de Brito, the wealthy rancher and senior town councillor, were Bahian-born. The chancellor of the High Court, Agostinho de Azevedo Monteiro, was married to a Brazilian. When he died he was replaced by Cristóvão de Burgos, a Bahian-born judge of the High Court. As historian Pedro Calmon points out, this was the first time that Brazilians predominated in the government of Brazil. The account presented here by Lopes Sierra is an "official" one and is interesting because it reveals for the first time the means by which the decision to form a triumvirate was made. It lacks, however, details of the political jockeying that had taken place when Afonso Furtado's death became imminent. Field Master Pedro Gomes, a sworn enemy of the governor, later argued that Afonso Furtado had risen from his deathbed to make sure that Gomes would be excluded from the junta (ANTT, Colecção São Vicente livro 13, fs. 270-72). Perhaps more important were the efforts of Bernardo Vieira Ravasco and the governor's nephew, Antônio de Sousa e Meneses, to prevent the purveyor, Antônio Lopes Ulhoa, from gaining the office of interim governor, which he coveted. It should also be noted that no representative of the church joined the junta, most likely owing to the fact that the bishop had died in 1672 and his replacement did not arrive until 1677. Aside from the manuscript sources cited above see Pedro Calmon, *História do Brasil*, 3:798-99, and the appendixes in Schwartz, *Sovereignty and Society in Colonial Brazil*, which provide some information on the High Court judges.

69. Afonso Furtado's death was reported to the Overseas Council in Portugal in the following manner by Antônio Lopes Ulhoa on 3 December 1675: "On the twenty-sixth of November the governor and captain general of this state Afonso Furtado de Mendonça died from a fever that began as erysipela and worsened to the point that no remedy or action could overcome it. He died with all the acts of religion and signs of predestination and because he was always moved by the zeal for His Highness's service, before dying he saw to the form in which this Government should remain after his death, calling together for this purpose the ministers of the High Court, all the officers of the city council of this city, the prelates of the Religious Orders, the senior officers of the militia, the Royal Treasurer, and some citizens and nobles." AHU, Bahia, *papéis avulsos*, caixa 12, 1st series uncataloged.

70. The "house of Bedão" in the text refers to the biblical incident when King David moved the ark from the house of Obed-edom to Jerusalem (2 Sam. 6:12-16).

71. The original Church and Convent of São Francisco was built in Salvador between

1587 and 1596. It was here that Afonso Furtado was interred. In 1686, however, the governor of Brazil, the Marquês das Minas, initiated construction of a new church and convent on the same site. This was completed and in use by 1713. Thus, the present Church of São Francisco occupies the location of Afonso Furtado's tomb but it postdates his burial. See Ferreira, *Memoria*, pp. 300-301.

72. By tradition the Carmelite Order traced its origins to the Prophet Elias. However, there is no historical evidence to support that connection. Instead, Berthold (died c. 1195), a relative of the Patriarch Aymeric, formed a congregation of religious on the slopes of Mount Carmel of which he became its first superior. Since the eighteenth century a bitter controversy has raged over the true relationship of the Carmelite Order to the Prophet Elias. See *Butler's Lives of the Saints*, Herbert Thurston and Donald Attwater, eds. (New York, 1956), 1:701-2, and Antonio Gavin, *A Short History of Monastical Orders* (London, 1693), pp. 153-57.

73. Tethys, in Greek mythology, the daughter of Earth and Heaven, sister and consort of Ocean and mother of rivers.

74. See note 72 above.

75. Funeral litter.

76. *Praça de terreiro* refers to the large plaza in front of the Jesuit Church of Salvador. Except for the square in front of the governor's palace and the town hall this was and is the most important place of public meeting in Salvador.

77. Although an artisan, Manuel Álvares Milão was admitted to the Misericórdia as a brother of superior condition in 1678. See Neuza Rodrigues Esteves, *Irmãos da Santa Casa de Misericórdia da Bahia* (Salvador, 1977), p. 102.

78. João de Almeida was an Englishman whose name was probably John May. He came to Brazil in 1588 and entered the Jesuit order in 1592. After extensive missionary work he served in the Jesuit College in Rio de Janeiro from 1639 until his death in 1653. He was confessor to Salvador Correia de Sá and other important people of Rio de Janeiro and after his death there was a movement for his beatification. His life was celebrated by Father Simão de Vasconcelos in his *Vida do Padre Joam d'Almeida, da Companhia de Iesu, na provincia do Brasil* (Lisbon, 1658). See also Charles R. Boxer, *Salvador de Sá and the Struggle for Brazil and Angola 1602-1686* (London, 1952), pp. 87-89.

79. Frei Cosme da São Damão (1574-1659) served as provincial of the Franciscan Order from 1657 to 1659. For a short biography see Basílio Röwer, *A ordem franciscana no Brasil* (Rio de Janeiro, 1947), pp. 172-78.

80. Jacinto Freire de Andrada, *Vida de Dom João de Castro quarto vizo-rei da India* (Lisbon, 1651). There is a modern edition by Justino Mendes de Almeida published by the Agência-Geral do Ultramar (Lisbon, 1968).

81. Don Juan de Palafox y Mendoza (1600-1659), bishop of Puebla de los Angeles and viceroy of New Spain (Mexico), June to November 1642, was a particularly controversial figure because of his struggle with the mendicant orders over control of the Indian population and his disputes with the Jesuits over tithes. In these matters, especially the control of the Indian population, he clashed with the duke of Escalona, the first grandee to be viceroy of New Spain. Eventually, Palafox succeeded in having Escalona removed from office in 1642. Lopes Sierra leaves the name of the author of the book on Palafox blank, but it almost surely was Antonio González de Rosende, a Franciscan friar minor

whose *Vida i virtudes del ill^{mo} i exc^{mo} señor D. Ivan de Palafox i Mendoza* was first published in Madrid in 1666 and then appeared in a second, amended edition in 1671. See Charles E. P. Simmons, "Palafox and his Critics: Reappraising a Controversy," *Hispanic American Historical Review* 46 (November, 1966):394-408. For a description of Palafox's activities see J. I. Israel, *Race, Class, and Politics in Colonial Mexico* (Oxford, 1975), pp. 200-216. The editor is indebted to Professor J. S. Cummins of the University of London for generous assistance in identifying González de Rosende as the author of the work mentioned by Lopes Sierra.

82. See page 45.

83. The Casa da India in Lisbon was the customs house and board of trade for the colonies. The buildings of the Casa da India were destroyed in 1755 by the great earthquake.

Acrostic poem from the manuscript "Paneguirico funebre" in the Biblioteca da Ajuda, Lisbon

Asnuas memorias de S.or Afonço Furtado de Castro Rios de Mendonça q. foi Cap.am general do Estado do Brazil E nas honrras q. em S.
Fran.co lhe fizerão em dous justos æpythos com huã jexma no meyo
con q. seja justa o nome do sujeito, Começando todos os principios ╪ A.M.M.M.
acabando nos ultimos seg.do se empresta, p.a oc.bruno Escrivães.

Soneto.

Applica — Augusta — Afabrica — Artificosa
Forasteyro — Flores — Fermosas — Flores,
Funçoins — Funebres. — Feitas — Se cum Favores
O grande, — O forte, — O sabio, — Officiosa.

Não — Notes — Nella — Nada majestosa
Ser — Sendo breve — Sinco ou — Seis Camões
O templo — O tecto, — O olio, — Ôs Escultores,
Fazendo — Fea — Fabrica — Fermosa

Venera — V.milde, — Vence — V mano risco
Reverente — Respeita, e — Rende — Roto
Teu — Talhe — Coração — Tristezas — Tea...

Acrostic poem from the manuscript "Paneguirico funebre"
in the Biblioteca da Ajuda, Lisbon

Index

INDEX

Acrostic poems, in Ajuda manuscript, 192n2, 203, 204-5
Address, forms of, 192-93n7
Afonso VI, 19, 193n7
Aimoré Indians, 9, 10, 193n10
Ajuda manuscript, 24, 191-92n2, 193n7, 195n28. *See also* Acrostic poems
Alagoas, 190n50
Alexander, emperor, 33, 88-89
Alexander III (the Great), 38, 192n4
Alexander Severus (Marcus Aurelius), 38, 192n4
Allegory: of heavens as the prince, 140-42; of men as stars, 155-56
Almeida, João de, 202n78
Almeida, Pedro de, 22, 200n63
Altaíde, Jerônimo de, 30, 115
Álvares, Diogo, "Caramurú," 169
Álvares Milão, Manuel, 128, 202n77
Amaro, João, 11-12
Amaro Maciel Parente, João, 48; biographical sketch of, 159-60
Amazon River, 5
Ameixal, 18
Amethysts, 54, 61, 62, 195n25
Angola, 44; governor of sends princes to Brazil, 23; ships sent to, 46

Apollo, oracle of, 113
Aporá, 57, 90, 187n3; Indian attacks on, 10
Aranha Pacheco, Nicolão, 59-60, 161, 196n31
Araújo e Lima, Sebastião de, 67, 75; letter to Lopes Sierra, 143-44
Arawak language, 197n39
Argos, 40, 192n5
Astrologers, 155
Atouguia, count of. *See* Altaíde, Jerônimo de
Augustus Caesar, 40
Avila, Garcia d', 169
Aviz, Order of. *See* Order of Aviz
Aymeric, 202n72
Azevedo, Álvaro de, 105, 125, 199n56, 201n68
Azevedo Monteiro, Agostínho de, 105, 201n68

Bahia, 16, 54, 86, 147, 159-69 *passim*, 174, 195n21, 196n34, 197n40; attacked by Indians, 6; captaincy of, 6, 8, 193n9; city council of, 14; Dellon's description of, 10; Jesuit College at, 163, 200n66; literary community in, 27; procession at, 51; Recôncavo of,

INDEX

175; sertão of, 10, 192n6; sugar in, 5, 13-14; weights, measures, and currency in, 182-83
Bandeiras. See Entradas
Banners, 121, 122, 124
Barbacena, 17, 18
Barbalho, Luís, 54
Barbosa, Francisco, 47; house of, 57, 69
Barbosa Calheiros, Domingos, 11
Barbosa de Araújo, family, 161
Barbosa de Mesquita, Manoel, 43, 193n*10*
Barcelona, 193n*12*
Baroque style, in art and literature, 26-27
Barreto de Meneses, Francisco, 43, 57, 63, 115
Bay of All Saints, 8, 160, 169, 193n*9*
Beira, 18
Berthold, 202n*72*
Biton, 40, 192n*5*
Blessed Sacrament, 49, 52, 60, 61, 99
Boqueirão, 171
Borba Gato, Manuel da, 163
Botelho de Oliveira, Manuel, 27, 29
Bragança, Catherine of, 64, 196n*36*
Brasilico, 197n*39*
Brazil: coastal settlement of, 4; colonial difficulties of, 14; economy of, 13-14; military organization in, 173-77; royal highway in, 43-44
Brazil Company, 160
Brazilwood trees, 4, 8, 15
Burgos, Cristovão de, 25, 194n*13*, 201n*68*

Caatinga, 197n*41*
Cabido, 50, 194n*19*
Cachoeira, 47, 66, 67, 87, 166, 170; overrun by Indians, 43; Paulistas arrive at, 57; ships sent to, 49; as staging area for expeditions, 8, 90
Cairú, 9, 11, 43, 160, 193n*10*
Calmon, Pedro, 201n*68*
Camamú, 9, 43, 168
Câmara: of Bahia, 14, 166; of Salvador, 168, 196n*35*
Camisão, 12
Campo Mayor, 18

Canary Islands, 54
Capanema, 10, 43
Cape of Good Hope, 54
Captaincies, 4-5
Carajá language, 197n*39*
Caravatá, 70, 197n*42*
Cardoso, Feliciano, 48
Cardoso, Luís, 46
Carib language, 197n*39*
Carmel, convent of Our Lady of, 72, 128
Carmelite Order, 202n*72*
Carvalho, Jeronimo, 54
Casa da India, 150, 203n*83*
Cassius, 38
Castel Melhor, count of, 115, 193n*7*
Castelo Branco, Pedro, 142
Castelo Branco, Rodrigo de, 29, 80, 81, 82, 93, 147, 196n*34*; arrival at Bahia, 74, 162; biographical sketch of, 162-63; and silver mines, 25, 74, 76, 85, 146, 162
Castro, João de, 144
Castro do Rio, Diogo de, 17
Catalonia, 198n*49*
Catholicism, post-Tridentine, 26
Cattle, 9, 10; sugar industry's need for, 5
Caturo, 148
Ceará, 11
Cesar, Luís, 151
Charles II, 196n*36*
Charles V, 39
Christ, Order of. *See* Order of Christ
Cleobis, 40, 192n*5*
Cochos Indians, 79, 198n*52*
Colbert, Jean Baptiste, 15
Colônia do Sacramento, 17
Comarcas, 193n*9*
Companhia Geral de Comércio do Brasil, 85, 148, 199-200n*57*
Contas River, 92, 200n*58*
Córdoba, customs house at, 199n*54*
Corsairs, 199n*55*
Costa, Manuel da, 69
Costa Barreto, Roque da, 22, 171
Covilhã, 31
Cristo, Lázaro de, 136

INDEX 211

Croesus, 39-40
Curitiba, Paraná, 200n61
Currency, table of, 183
Cuzco, 162

Dampier, William, 174
David, 75, 115, 116, 201n70
De sangue illustre, 198n48
De sangue limpio, 198n48
Death, as symbol in baroque tradition, 26
Dellon, Gabriel, 10
Delphi, 192n5
Destêrro, convent of, 171
Diamonds, 12, 13
Dias, Henrique, 175
Dias Adorno, Gaspar, 10
Dias d'Avila, Francisco, 25
Dias Laços, Tomé, 10
Dias Pais, Fernão, 25, 163
Dowries, 59, 61, 161
Duarte Caturo, Manuel, 87
Dutch, 10, 14, 15, 29, 170, 174, 176; armada, 41
Dyewood. *See* Brazilwood trees

Ecclesiasticus, 139
Elias, 202n72
Elvas, 17, 19
Emboabas, War of the, 160
Emeralds, 13; mountain of, 25, 163
Engenhos, 5
English, 14
Entradas: against the Indians, 16-17, 64-65, 159, 175-76; cost of supplies for, 66-67; for mineral wealth, 6, 71, 175-76
Ericeira, count of, 19
Erysipelas, 95-96, 200n63, 200n64
Esau, 53
Escalona, duke of, 202n81
Escragnolle Taunay, Afonso de, 12
Espirito Santo, 6, 25
Esquife, 122, 124, 202n75
Estremoz, 18
Evora, 18

Faia, Inácio, 51, 137
Ferreira, Carlos Alberto, 23
Ferreira Soares, Antônio, 194n18
Ferrera, 18
Fidalgo, 164; *da casa*, 198n48
Figueredo, Francisco de, 80
Figueriedo, Agostinho de, 96, 200n61
Firewood, used in sugar industry, 9, 11
Fortresses, 42
Franciscan Order, 202n79
Freire de Andrada, Jacinto, 144, 189n27, 202n80
French, 4
Frontera, Marqués de, 54
Funeral: in literature, 24; as popular event, 26
Furtado de Castro do Rio de Mendonça, Afonso, 16, 114, 159, 194n18; administration of, 20, 22, 23, 46, 88-90, 113-16, 145-46, 164, 174; arrival of, at Salvador, 45; biography of, 17-23; charity of, 49, 56, 57, 99, 106, 113, 114, 115, 150; consultations with, 21, 45, 49, 98, 99, 102-3; death of, 20, 26, 38, 93, 109, 112, 145, 150, 151-52, 201n68, 201n69; and Dom Pedro de Almeida, 22; family of, 17, 20, 114, 170-72, 193n11, 199n56; funeral of, 99, 100, 116-18, 119, 120, 122, 123, 124-27, 128, 129-35, 201-2n71; genealogy of, 180-81; as governor, 14, 18, 39, 40, 99; illness of, 67-69, 94-97, 105-6, 127, 200n63; and Indians, 10, 20-23, 54, 64-66, 73-74, 166, 168; military career of, 17-20, 38, 46, 114, 176; and mines, 13, 54, 61, 94, 145, 146, 148-49, 152, 154, 162, 163; orders of, 46, 50-52, 196n34; and Pedro II, 19, 25, 154, 195n25, 196n26; prayers of, 84, 100-101, 107-8, 110, 112; property of, 18, 19; and rebellion of Sergipe de El-Rey, 46, 194n14; and Relação, 25; religiosity of, 20, 49, 98, 116, 138-39; and religious orders, 17, 57, 58, 76, 84, 115, 195n28, 198n49; reprimands governor of Pernambuco,

21; reprimands town council of Porto Seguro, 21; rivals of, 145-52; and settlement of Boqueirão, 171; and ship repairs, 55-56, 79-80; speeches of, 63, 68, 103-4; successor to, 102-3, 105; suppression of escaped slaves by, 21, 22-23; titles, grants of, 19, 20, 31
Furtado de Mendonça, João, 18, 20, 83-84, 145, 171-72, 174, 199n56, 201n67
Furtado de Mendonça, Jorge (father of Afonso), 17
Furtado de Mendonça, Jorge (son of Afonso), 18, 20, 84, 199n56

Galachos Indians, 25
Gama, Francisco da, 56
Gê language, 197n39
General Company of Commerce of Brazil, 85, 148, 199-200n57
Goa, archbishop of, 54
Gold, 4, 12, 13, 15-16, 17, 82, 160, 163
Gomes, Pedro, 43-44, 57, 125, 161, 174, 195n27, 199n56; biographical sketch of, 170-72
Gonçalves Freitas, Manuel, 48
González de Rosende, Antonio, 202n81
Granada, 28, 52, 195n24
Graniça, João de, 81, 147
Grens Indians, 9
Guedes de Brito, Antônio, 47, 68, 105, 114, 194n15, 201n68; biographical sketch of, 168-70
Gusmão, Alexandre de, 97-98, 100, 106-7, 200-201n66

Habit of Christ, 47
Hannibal, 38
"Henriques," 175
Herodotus, 191n1, 192n5
Holland, peace of, 64
Holy House of Mercy. *See* Misericórdia
Homer, 34, 39
House of India, 150, 203n83

Ilhéus, 6, 8-9, 10, 43, 160
Indians: attacks of, 6, 10, 11, 43; captive, 6, 12, 78, 197-98n45; classification of by Portuguese, 197n39; and colonization, 5-6; and commerce, 65; conquest of, 10-11, 71-72; expeditions against, 25, 175-76, 192n6; friendly, 67, 68, 72, 73; as laborers, 198n51; languages of, 5, 6, 197n39; peace mission of, 70; as soldiers, 175. *See also* specific Indian groups
Inojosa, Manuel de, 48, 67, 79, 86-87, 90, 92, 198n52, 200n58
Inquisition, 166
Itabaiana, mountains of, 74, 76, 80, 162
Itapecuru River, 169
Itaporá, 187n3
Itapororocas, 10, 11

Jacob, 53
Jacobina, 10, 11, 68, 169, 197n40
Jacuasui, 71
Jacuipe River, 166
Jaguaripe, 8, 10, 43
Jesuits, 6, 138, 195n21, 195n22, 200n66, 202n81; colleges of, 26, 163, 165, 200n66, 202n78
Jiquiriça, 10, 11
João IV, 17, 29, 95, 115, 142, 150, 196n36, 200n62; letter of, 154; speech of, 151
João V, 176
João Amaro, 12, 159
Joiaicà Capitua Topins, 71
Jonah, 49, 50
Joshua, 115
Julius Caesar, 38
Junta de Comércio, 200n57

Laval, Pyrard de, 16
Lazaro, Frei, 109-10
Lemos, Manuel de, 70
Lima, Francisco de, 50
Lingua geral, 197n39
Lingua travada, 197n39
Lisbon, 15, 83, 88, 162, 164, 195n22, 196n32
Livy, 192n3

INDEX

Lopes Sierra, Juan, 3, 4, 27-30, 31, 35, 36, 37, 201n67; and *Anticatastrophe* fragment, 28; as author of "Paneguirico funebre," 28-30, 33-36, 112, 143-44, 156; in Granada, 28, 52, 195n24; in Seville, 28, 82-83
Lopes Sierra, Juan, manuscript. *See* "Paneguirico funebre"
Lopes Ulhoa, Antônio, 51, 201n68, 201n69
Luba, Gaspar, 48
Luso-Dutch War, 14, 15, 29, 170

Madeira, 54
Madrid, 52
Magellan, 92, 150
Malachite, 13
Manicongo, 193n11
Manioc, 8, 9, 11, 199n57
Manuel I, 150
Maracás Indians, 12, 76, 77, 78-79, 90, 170
Maracavaçus Indians, 11
Maragogipe, 8, 10, 22, 160
Maranhão, 189n27
Maré, island of, 160
Maroon community, 190n50
Marques de Perada, Antônio, 24
Massacará, 12
Mata de São João, 169
Mata seca, 197n41
Matos, Francisco de, 51, 195n22
Matos de Aguiar, João de, 47-49, 66, 167-68, 196n37
Matos e Guerra, Gregório de, 26, 27, 28, 29, 163
May, John. *See* Almeida, João de
Mazagão, 192n6
Measures, table of, 182
Mello, Francisco Manuel de, 29, 95, 163, 193n12, 200n62
Melo e Castro, Antônio de, 41, 42, 193n8
Mendes, Francisco, 48
Mercantilism, 15
Mestiços, 6

Mexico, 202n81; viceroy of, 145
Milão, Manuel Álvares, 128
Military organization, Brazilian and Portuguese, 173-77
Minas, Marquês de, 24, 202n71
Minas Gerais, 9, 11, 17, 25, 26, 160, 163
Mineral wealth, search for, 6, 10, 12, 13, 16, 25, 175-76
Mines: and "patio process," 162; reports on, 83, 87-88. *See also* Amethysts, Diamonds, Emeralds, Gold, Saltpeter, Silver
Minho, 165, 167
Misericórdia, Brotherhood of the, 29, 124, 126, 166, 168, 195n29, 196n33, 198n50, 202n77; Holy House, 26, 57, 59, 60-61, 124, 195n29; purveyor of, 57, 59, 161, 164, 169, 170
Moço fidalgo, 198n48
Monomotapa, 15, 16
Monsoon, 55
Montserrate, Benedictine monastery of, 193n12
Montserrate, Nossa Senhora de, 45, 75-76, 83, 95, 193n12, 198n49
Moors, 83
Morro do Chapéu, 169
Mota, Vasco da, 48
Mourão, 18
Munhos, João, 194n14

Nabo Pasanha, Antônio, 105
New Christians, 166, 167, 194n18, 198n50
Nineveh, 49
Nossa Senhora da Boa Memoria, 87
Nossa Senhora de Montserrate. *See* Montserrate, Nossa Senhora de
Nossa Senhora de Oliveira, 87
Nossa Senhora do Rosario e São Caetano, 79-80

Óbidos, conde de, 115
Odivelas, 50, 194n18
Olivença, 18, 19
Oporto, 83
Orange, Prince of, 52

Ordenanças, 175-76
Orobó, 69, 90; fort of, 10-11, 43-44, 57, 63; mountains, 170, 171-72
Order of Aviz, 194n*16*
Order of Christ, 17, 19, 31, 117, 160, 168, 169, 170, 194n*16*
Order of Santiago, 59, 168, 194n*16*
Order of São Francisco, 138
Order of Templars, 194n*16*
Otinga. *See* Utinga
Overseas Council, 20, 22, 201n*69*

Paço de Arcos, 54
Pactá, 86
Paes de Sande, Antônio, 162
Paiäiäs Indians, 10, 11, 47, 67, 166, 187n*6*, 194n*15*, 197n*40*
Palafox y Mendoza, Juan de, 145, 202-3n*81*
Palmares, 21, 22-23, 190n*50*, 196n*34*
Palo blando, 69, 197n*41*
Panacu, 73, 198n*46*
"Paneguirico funebre," 20, 22, 159, 166, 170, 172, 176, 201n*68*, 202n*81*; content of, 9, 12, 24-27; letter criticizing, 143-44; manuscripts of, 24
Papal Bull, 109
Paraguaçu, 43
Paraguaçu River, 8, 12, 90, 115, 159, 166, 187n*3*
Paraguay, 6
Paraíba, 167
Paranaguá: mines of, 81, 84, 85, 93, 147, 162; mountains of, 80, 146, 154
Patatiba, 144
Paul, Saint, 37
Paulistas, 6, 11, 23, 44, 47-49, 63; in Cachoeira, 46-47, 57; in Ceará, 11; expeditions of, 6, 62, 64, 66, 69, 71-72, 76-79, 196n*37*; in Paraguay, 6; quarrel among themselves, 66-67; in Utinga, 70
Peace of Holland. *See* Holland, peace of
Pedro II, 53, 193n*7*; letter of, 154
Peixoto Viegas, João, 47, 81, 147, 169, 187n*6*, 194n*15*, 197n*40*; biographical sketch of, 165-67; mountains of, 85, 147; property of, 11, 162
Pernambuco, 5, 10, 13-14, 74, 86, 196n*34*; governor of, 21, 22, 200n*63*
Philip III, 52
Philip IV, 52-53, 195n*24*
Piguraça, mountains of, 61, 80
Pinto, Antônio, 197n*40*
Piranhas, 69, 70; fort of, 44, 57, 63
Pires, Francisco, 67
Pitta, Sebastião da Rocha, 19, 193n*10*
Plata River, 17, 176, 199n*54*
Plutarch, 38, 191n*1*, 200n*59*
Poison, 91, 197n*42*
Ponte, House of, 168
Ponte de Lima, 167
Porsenna, Lars, 192n*3*
Porto Seguro, 6, 10, 21
Portugal, 15, 17, 173; agrees to cede Tangier and Bombay to England, 196n*36*; grants captaincies in Brazil, 4; Overseas Council, 20, 22, 201n*36*
Post-Tridentine Catholicism, 26
Potosí, 12, 16, 81, 82, 150, 199n*54*
Printing press, 27
Processions, religious, 51, 72, 120-26
Puebla de los Angeles, 145, 202n*81*
Purificação, Frei Ínacio da, 137-38

Quitose River, 79, 86-87, 90, 91, 200n*58*

Rabello Leite, Jorge, 194n*14*
Ramires de Esquivel, Diogo, 87
Ravasco Cavalcanti e Albuquerque, Gonçalo, 163, 165
Real River, 9
Rebelo, Bento, 67
Recife, 195n*21*
Recôncavo, 8, 9, 11, 161, 167, 171, 175
Reis, Manuel dos, 83
Relação, 25, 50, 124, 172, 195n*20*
Restoration, War of, 18, 19, 20, 173, 196n*32*
Rio de Janeiro, 8, 81, 138, 171, 195n*21*; administrator from, 86; governor of, 199n*56*; Jesuit College in, 202n*66*,

202n78; purveyor of treasury at, 85, 147
Rio Grande do Norte, 167
Ribeiro Baião Parente, Estevão, 11-12, 48, 187n6, 194n17; biographical sketch of, 159-60
Rodrigues Adorno, Bras, 47, 57, 66, 67
Rodrigues Arzão, Bras, 11-12, 48, 159
Rodrigues Botão, Antônio, 87, 200n58
Rodrigues de Siqueira, João, 85
Royal High Court. See Relação
Royal Treasury, 62
Royal Tribunal of Justice. See Relação

Sá, family, 171
Sá, João Correia de, 54
Sá, Salvador Correia de, 22, 202n78
Sá Peixoto, Joana de, 166
Sabarabuçu, 25, 163
Sacambuaçu, 71, 73
Sacatín, 53
Sacred Company of Jesus, 51
Saint Francis, Third Order of. See Third Order of Saint Francis
Saltpeter, 54, 61, 62, 195n25, 196n34
Salvador (da Bahia de todos os Santos), 3, 11, 25, 31, 162, 165, 193n12, 195n26; architecture of, 26; authors in, 27-28, 163; Benedictines of, 198n49; expulsion of Dutch from, 174; finances of, 64, 92-93; founding of, 8; government of, 5, 169; Jesuit College at, 26, 165; religion in, 26
Sande, Francisca de, 61, 196n33
Santa Cruz, count of, 148
Santiago, Order of. See Order of Santiago
Santo Amaro, 8
Santo Antonio, fort of, 41
Santo Antônio da Conquista (João Amaro), 159, 198n52
Santos, Estevão dos, 60, 61, 196n32
Santos, port of, 5
São Bento, fort of, 119
São Cristovão, 9, 194n14
São Damão, Cosme da, 138, 202n79

São Francisco, church and convent of, 26, 120, 124, 126, 135, 196n32, 201-2n71
São Francisco, Order of. See Order of São Francisco
São Francisco River, 5, 9, 71, 160, 169, 170, 196n34
São João de Refriegas, 31
São Jorge dos Ilhéus, 9
São Julião de Bragança, 31
São Paulo, 6, 12, 16-17, 66, 162, 198n51
São Pedro de Rates, 54-56, 195n26
São Romão de Fonte Coberta, 31
São Vicente, 6, 80, 81, 85, 88, 149, 200n61; church of, 60; Indians sent to, 78; ministers of, 82, 146
São Vicente de Fora, church of, 196n32
Sapoiás Indians, 67, 197n40
Sardanapalus, 50
Sebastião, 17, 173
Sebola, 37, 192n3
Senado da Câmara, 50, 194n19
Sergipe de El-Rey, 9, 44-45, 146, 194n14; captain major of, 74; rebellion in, 42, 46, 192n6
Serra, João Lopes. See Lopes Sierra, Juan
Sertão, 5-6, 90, 92, 166
Sertão do baixo, 193n9
Sesmaria, 169, 170, 171
Setúbal, 170
Seville, 28, 52, 82-83
Ship repairs, 55-56, 79-80
Shipwreck, of João Furtado de Mendonça, 83-84
Silva Freitas, Manuel da, 62
Silver, 13, 15, 16, 25, 54, 74, 81, 145, 146, 195n25; mines, 61, 62, 93, 147, 162, 199n54
Sim, Francisco Fernandes do, 59-61, 116, 160-61, 196n30, 196n31
Slaves: African, 14, 15, 22; at Palmares, 21, 22-23, 190n50, 196n34; silver traded for, 16; in sugar fields and mills, 5
Smith, David, 161
Smuggling, 199n54
Soares de França, Gonçalo, 27

216 INDEX

Soares de Macedo, Jorge, 162
Soares Ferreira, Antônio, 48, 85
Solomon, 75, 115, 116, 142, 143
Solon, 39
Sonho, count of, 44, 193n*11*
Sonnet, affixed to mast of ship, 56
Sousa, Francisco de, 198n*49*
Sousa de Távora, Simão de, 79
Sousa e Meneses, Antônio de, 20, 106, 109, 135, 165, 171, 199n*56*, 201n*67*, 201n*68*; and Lopes Sierra manuscript, 24, 29, 33-34, 136
Sousa Freire, Alexandre de, 11, 40, 44, 60, 79, 115, 192n*6*, 196n*37*
Spanish, defeated, 176
Sugar, 4-5, 13-16, 167; in Bahia, 5, 13-14; in Ilhéus, 9; mills, 4, 65, 164, 169; in Pernambuco, 5, 13-14; in the Recôncavo, 8-9; near São Cristovão, 9; in Sergipe de El-Rey, 9
Sumidouro, 163
Suriel, Bento, 61-62, 80, 196n*34*

Tabaçú, 57, 58
Tapuyas, 197n*39*, 197n*40*
Távora, Francisco de, 44, 193n*11*
Távora, Magdalena de, 20, 199n*56*
Távora, María de, 20, 171-72, 199n*56*
Taxes, 14, 167, 200n*60*
Telles, Antônio, 46, 115
Telles de Meneses, Francisco, 165, 193n*13*
Telon, 40
Templars, Order of. *See* Order of Templars
Terço, system, 173-74
Terreiro, Square of the, 125, 202n*76*
Tethys, 122, 202n*73*
Third Order of Saint Francis, 61, 76, 169, 198n*50*
Tobias, 115
Topin, 70
Topinis Indians, 11
Topis Indians, 78
Tordesillas, Treaty of, 197n*44*

Treasury Board, 62-63
Tupí-Guaraní language, 5, 6, 197n*39*
Tupís Indians, 67
Turks, 84, 199n*55*
Tuxliman, 52

Utinga, 58, 70, 71, 197n*43*
Utinga River, 197n*43*

Vasconcelos, Simão de, 29, 138, 202n*78*
Vaz, Pedro, 11
Velho, Domingos Jorge, 196n*34*
Velho, Gaspar, 48
Velho de Lima, Sebastião, 80
Verde River, 54, 61, 80
Vereador, 196n*35*
Vergil, 34, 39
Viana do Castelo, 165
Victoria, 92
Viegas Xortes, João, 48
Vieira, Antônio, 26, 27, 162, 163, 164, 165, 196n*38*, 199n*55*
Vieira, João, 74, 76, 147
Vieira Ravasco, Bernardo, 27, 29, 67, 75, 102, 113, 166, 196n*38*, 201n*68*; biographical sketch of, 163-65
Vila Nova, countess of, 200n*62*
Vila Pouca, conde de, 54, 115
Vila Viçosa, 142, 143, 151
Vilas do Baixo, 193n*9*
Viriathus, 38, 192n*4*
Vitoria, church of, 74
Viva Rambla, Plaza of, 52

Weights, table of, 183
Whaling contract, 20, 199n*56*
Wine, 93, 199n*57*

Xerxes, 34

Zambezi River, 16
Zarza, 18
Zorilla, Rojas, 189n*31*